OUTSIDE THE CLASSROOM: RESEARCHING LITERACY WITH ADULT LEARNERS

edited by

F'.ayne Fowler and Jane Mace

niace

promoting adult learning

niace

promoting adult learning

© 2005 National Institute of Adult Continuing Education
(England and Wales)

21 De Montfort Street
Leicester
LE1 7GE
Company registration no. 2603322
Charity registration no. 1002775

NIACE has a broad remit to promote lifelong learning opportunities for
adults. NIACE works to develop increased participation in
education and training, particularly for those who do not have easy access
because of class, gender, age, race, language and culture, learning difficulties or disabilities, or insufficient financial resources.

You can find NIACE online at www.niace.org.uk

Cataloguing in Publication Data
A CIP record of this title is available from the British Library

ISBN 1 86201 223 7

Designed and typeset by Kerrypress Ltd, Luton
Printed and bound in the UK by Latimer Trend, Plymouth

Contents

Part II 'Practice'

Appendices

Acknowledgements

This book would not have been possible without the contributions of a large number of people including all of the trainees who took part in the pilot training courses and the literacy students who so generously shared their lives with us. Thank you one and all. We would also like to acknowledge the Oxford Brookes for designing the pilot Adult Literacy Specialist Courses in 2002/3 and Wiltshire and Swindon Learning and Skills Council for funding the courses.

In addition, special thanks are due to Keith and Matthew Fowler for enabling the writing and to Tim Parker for his great colour suggestions.

Introduction

Jane Mace

We can begin by saying that this book has two purposes: first, to bring to life a theory about the uses of literacy in adult life, and second, to show how this might illuminate teacher training and teaching practice.

However, this assertion seems to take for granted that theory and practice are separate matters, with a world of theory *over there* and another world of practice *over here* and light being shone in one direction only. The idea that theory might shed light on practice seems a bit of a one-way street. The separation of practice from theory itself seems an over-simplification. In reality, any teacher, whether consciously or not, will have some theory of learning lurking somewhere in their heads, even if they have not articulated this out loud.

Nevertheless it is also true that a lot of effort at theory does go on in a different world from teaching practice. Theory-workers and teachers do not always know each other very well; they might not even recognise each other in the street. While theory and practice cannot be neat compartments, it remains the case that researchers graft away to publish work in all sorts of fields that teachers could find it useful to read and learn from. Equally, there are some things that good teachers may already know intuitively and could sometimes encourage researchers to notice from a pedagogical perspective.

A good example of this is the concept of literacy as a social practice, at the heart of this book. Adult literacy teachers know that their job is to enhance reading and writing outside the context of classroom, but its constraints require them to spend a great deal of time having to think about literacy as *skills*; so that there is a risk that they might teach skills out of the context in which anyone uses them (or rather, only in the context of classroom use). Meanwhile, academic researchers have been developing a view of literacy as *practice* – a cultural activity in a cultural space – and they too have to beware of a risk: this time, that of making the idea sound very abstract, too 'theoretical.' Both teachers and researchers, incidentally, are practitioners – but practitioners of teaching can understandably feel a little impatient with theory that has no immediate sign of helping the kind of practice they are paid to think about.

The two of us have had the good fortune to move between both worlds. Our working lives have included both research and teaching. We are members of a twenty-year-old network of researcher-practitioners in adult literacy (RaPAL 2005). In our wish to explore how the idea of literacy practice may help enrich and enhance the reality of teaching practice, we have trained teachers to become researchers: and it is from the work produced in that training that the idea of this book was born.

The task of undertaking and reporting on a research project into literacy as a social practice was an assignment we designed as part of this training. The focus had to be: a case study of an adult literacy learner. Reading the case study reports that resulted was unlike any other reading we had done of teachers describing students. In itself, that felt like the basis of work that was worth publishing. At the same time, in teaching these assignments, we had found no other published guide which brought 'theory' and 'practice' together (the scare quotes persist); and there seemed the need for some writing about this from us. Since an appreciation of *context* is a key element in the social practice view of literacy, it seems important here to summarise something of that within which our work developed from those initial ideas.

Changes

Things have changed a lot in British adult literacy education since the 'Right to Read' campaign of the 1970s. In fact, since the 1990s, there has been nothing short of a revolution. Where once there was little research and patchy training, both research and training have come to life and proliferated. The year 1997 saw a newly-elected Labour government having to put flesh on manifesto promises to do something about adult basic skills, and in the next few years reports, committees and funding agencies duly delivered. A 'national' strategy was agreed, with targets. But the word 'national' itself carried a new meaning; for 1997 also saw devolved government emerging for Wales, Scotland and Ireland. This book contains experience and analysis drawn from *English,* not British adult literacy work. The subject specifications on which training courses for teachers have been set up and which drive the design and funding of qualifications for those teachers are specifications which apply to *English* adult literacy teachers, not those in Scotland, Wales or Ireland. Given the way the word 'national' is scattered around policy documents from the English Department for Education and Skills (formerly DfEE), this is important to stress. As the National Literacy Trust has pointed out, the press, taking their cue from this, has tended to write ever since as if every announcement from the DfES were statutory throughout the UK (cited in Hamilton, Macrae and Tett, 2001: 40). Their 'key milestones' offer a useful picture of how the nation began to divide as policy developed:

> 1998 ***England and Wales:*** *Government asked Lord Moser to report on how to tackle poor basic skills.*

Scotland: Lifelong Learning paper issued.

1999 **England and Wales:** *A Fresh Start (the Moser Report) stated that 7 million adults have literacy and numeracy difficulties and made recommendations.*

2000 **England:** *Department of Education and Skills established Adult Basic Skills Strategy Unit to implement these.*

Scotland: adult literacy task force launched.

2001 **England**: *Government launched Skills for Life, national strategy for improving adult literacy and numeracy skills [eds: and Basic Skills Agency published English literacy core curriculum]*

Wales: *National Basic Skills Strategy (as part of the Learning Country) asked Basic Skills Agency to develop a curriculum for adults.*

Scotland: adult literacy drive launched.

(*NLT 2004*)

Lyn Tett, Catherine Macrae and Mary Hamilton offer a useful comparative account of the different ways in which policy emerged and began to be implemented. These were two differences they found, among others. In England and Wales, there seems to be a strong emphasis on standardised tests and learner qualifications; whereas in Scotland, some energy seems to have been directed at outcomes which may be seen as more social and collective. In Ireland the National Adult Literacy Agency had maintained a practice of carrying out consultations with learners and feeding these back to government, seen by some to be in contrast with a more top-down approach from the Basic Skills Agency in England and Wales. (Hamilton, Macrae and Tett)

There was one thing that developments in all four countries seem to have had in common, however:

> '*In none of these settings does there appear to be a strong professional voice moderating the official policy agenda. This is in contrast to what has happened in school-based reforms in the past 10 years, where teachers have influenced the new assessment and curricula.*' (ibid.: 37)

Adult literacy teachers and learners were somewhat left out in this period of committees and agendas. And the funding regime which followed has not helped foster a feeling of recognition for inventive work in the classroom. As Peter Lavender has pointed out, when financial rewards follow successful achievement of targets, it makes for a rather narrow view of who is to be taught and with what purposes. (Lavender 2004)

Change often brings contradictions and these new developments have been no exception. Although there has been a sense of growth and attention that had been lacking in the 1980s, many teachers and managers have complained of inordinate demands for paperwork. It took time for the new core curriculum (BSA 2001) to be seen as guide rather than rulebook, and even now the inexperienced teacher too often sees it as a prescriptive solution to their uncertainties. The major counter-point to all this, however, has undoubtedly been the liberation offered by a supported research culture, complete with a whole new infrastructure. The National (sic) Research and Development Centre for literacy, numeracy and language has produced an impressive range of activity since its foundation in 2001 and high on its stated agenda are both the learners and teachers who had been hitherto so neglected. These are the first three items in the list of 'values and principles that underpin' what the Centre does:

- to ensure that the needs of learners are the central focus of our work

- to address equality and diversity in all our activities

- to engage practitioners in all stages of our work. (NRDC n.d.: 14)

Reports and conferences, projects and programmes have proliferated. And the issue of how to ensure critical and active participation by adult learners is a live topic of debate (Tomlin 2004). It is in this context that the new training and staff development courses for adult literacy teachers have been emerging, since the Further Education National Training Organisation produced a set of specifications for adult literacy teachers: a list of things the specialist in this field needs to show she knows about if she is to be properly qualified. (FENTO 2002)

As far as we know, no-one has ever publicly claimed authorship of these 'subject specifications.' Like the others for teachers of numeracy and ESOL, these are texts published as government documents, and government documents keep personalities out of it. We suspect that many adult literacy trainers, academics and administrators would like to have had the chance to sit down with the author(s) and ask them a few questions. (For example: how was it that you thought an adult literacy teacher's first task should be to deal with phonetics?) For many organisa-tions and individuals struggling to translate them into courses which could then carry the approval and therefore cachet of a national accreditation, they seemed to have the effect of headlights on a rabbit. With the passage of time, however, curriculum designers and trainers have recovered our confidence and have applied ourselves to putting flesh on the basic skeleton, so that at the time of writing more than two dozen 'level 4' courses are now on offer across England, all with the imprimatur of FENTO approval, and all slightly different from each other in emphasis and texture.

In brief this is what the specifications require. A specialist adult literacy teacher needs to have knowledge and skills in two areas: first, a theoretical and conceptual awareness of English language development and use and second, a high level of skill in their own literacy. The first, major area, and the one that concerns us in this book, contains three lists, known in the trade as: linguistics, learning and context. This represents a striking invitation: *one third* of the main content of the training has to focus on 'the factors that influence or shape the use of language and literacy' (*op. cit.*: 13).

Teachers and learners

Within such a context, this book fits with the NRDC's call for a focus on learners. The stories (or portraits) that follow each result from teachers seeking out and working with men and women currently studying literacy, and exploring with them something of their reading and writing lives outside the classroom. By definition, this project positioned the learner as expert. Each consented to give their time and each had varied amount of input in what was written. As we shall see, their responses to this participation were also various: including passive acceptance, kindly helpfulness, active curiosity and interest. We have been careful in what we claim to have been the project's value or benefit to them. Some made no particular comment about what they had gained from it. Just a few, however, were really struck by a new insight it had given them. Suddenly, instead of seeing themselves merely in terms of being 'poor' at reading or spelling, 'no good' at dealing with paperwork, 'not up to much' in their individual skills, they saw something different.

Each of the nineteen contributors you will meet in the coming pages therefore is writing about a research relationship with their subject. They carried out various kinds of interview; they visited places they were told about; they supported their subject in writing their own written sketch of themselves. They also connected what they learned with what they had read from the literature. But perhaps the hardest bit of all was that they then sat down and wrote about the person, trying to keep faith with what they had been told, and struggling to convey something of their vitality on the page; translating what had been dialogue and chat into a silent, written, 'case study' – to then be read as an assessable piece of work.

Structure

The book is arranged as follows. In the first part on 'theory', we look at the three aspects of the social practice view of literacy:

- the idea of *literacy events* – observable moments when people are doing reading or writing, as part of something else (and the *literacy practices* of which they form a part);

- then, that of *social networks* – which shift over time and support or inhibit our uses of literacy; and

- thirdly, the concept of the *literacy environment* that we inhabit at a given time or place: partly, but not wholly, expressed by the physical presence of texts around us.

In each of the three sections, a group of portraits follows an introduction to the topic discussed, each of which illustrates different ways in which that aspect may feature in a person's social interactions.

In the second part of the book, we look at two aspects of 'practice': research and teaching. The first section sets out something of the process of doing the research, illustrated with another group of portraits, each with a different nuance on the research relationship. The second brings together the strands of thinking employed in undertaking these projects and signals further directions for teaching and research.

In order to share the source of this work we have included, in Appendix one, an account of the original assignment and guidelines as delivered in the training. Appendix two provides the letter of permission that was sent to participants.

Editing

There are two main tasks we have undertaken as editors. One has been to engage with the authors in the work of transforming essays written as assessment tasks into essays written as part of a book; the other, to work with each other in writing our own contributions. Until July 2003 what we could call our literacy relationship with the authors had been as their course tutors (and assessors). From November, when they accepted our invitation to take part in this project, this changed. We were asking their permission to use their work. The subjects of their pieces also had to be consulted; and the authors were asked to check with them their willingness to be included. (See Appendix 2).

The first main change we made to the essays, as editors, was to cut one of the very elements the authors had been required to include in order for their essays to pass on the course: namely, references to, and quotes from other sources. We did this to avoid the book becoming tedious for you, the reader, so that you would not have to keep seeing similar passages quoted and the same four or five sources referred to. These are sources we discuss (with others) in our own essays in each section.

The second change we made was to translate all the narratives in the essays from the present tense into the past. Typically (and rightly) essay-writers had described their subjects as very much in the here and now. 'John lives with his fiancée'; 'Ruth is a 50-year-old woman'; 'Vicky works as a groom'; 'Now, Tony writes daily; he can see the improvements'. To have written these in the past about John or Ruth or Vicky or Tony, who were all very much alive to their authors in classroom or the local community, would have been somewhat macabre. Our use of the past tense for publication, however, acknowledges that life moves on, and that change may have taken place in any of the circumstances described. It also situates the people (and their conversations with their interviewers) in a historical context.

As to our own contributions for the book, we were both drawing on the teaching and reading that remains part of work we both do. The listening and talking we did at our meetings helped us each to return to the writing. Collaboration has been the key to it at every stage; but since we each took responsibility for drafting different chapters, you will find that each has the individual name of its author beside it.

Chapter 1

Events, practices and values

Jane Mace

Like 'culture', the closer a 'literacy practice' is, the harder it can be to see it. It is just how life is: it is normal. Once we distance ourselves from it, however, we can recognise it more clearly as something specific to a particular time and place, which has not always been so and is not so everywhere else. You and I, for example, may find it hard to imagine life when writing felt *less important* than speech. Yet in medieval Europe, people would never have dreamed of seeing a mere piece of writing as sufficient to carry legal authority. At such a time, for an oath, promise or contract to have legal validity, it had to be uttered in the presence of witnesses. The more solemn the decision – whether sale of land or bequest of an honour – the less writing had a place. Even if a document was produced, the important part of it was the seal which was put on it; and a seal could have significance in its own right, without the document.[1] The feeling of the time was that 'the true facts of a transaction were engraved on the hearts and minds of the witnesses and *could not be fully recorded in writing* however detailed.' (my italics) (Clanchy 1979: 207). At that time in Europe, legal literacy practices laid greater emphasis on the authority of the present witness than on the symbolic mark of their presence provided by their cross or signature. Writing and reading were an adjunct, even an optional extra, to the spoken word and the act of speaking (*ibid*: 207–210).

Set against this background, the stress on evidence in writing which prevails in industrialised countries today looks remarkable. This is neither 'natural' nor 'normal': it is the product of a particular time: a distinct literacy practice which carries consequences for the distribution of power. Texts are a primary source of our very identity. You can be reminded of this if you have to deal with the paperwork of moving house, as I was while writing this chapter. Among the letters and documents I had to read and documents I had to sign was a flyer sent

---

[1] During this period, however, things were changing: the power of both church and text were growing. A story is told of a group of men being tried on a charge of heresy. They made the mistake, in court, of sneering at the book-learning of the clergy who were cross-examining them: learning which, they said, was nothing more than the product of human 'fabrications' 'written on the skins of animals' – in contrast to 'the law written in the inner many by the Holy Spirit' on which their own beliefs were founded. For this, their punishment was to be burnt at the stake. (Clanchy 1979: 207)

to me by my solicitor, produced by The Law Society, headed with the question: 'Using a solicitor?'. This explained the new measures that had recently come into force, designed to make it more difficult for those known as money launderers (criminals who disguise stolen money as legitimate income by using an assumed identity):

> *Banks and building societies have had to check the identity of customers for some time. Now solicitors have to. This means you will have to show your solicitor, or somebody acting on their behalf, some personal documentation.*
> (Law Society leaflet, no date)

Examples of this personal documentation were the usual ones: current signed passport, birth certificate, utility bill, driving licence with photocard. The words in the last line of the leaflet are striking:

> *'If you don't have these documents, you will have to ask your solicitor to advise you on **how best to prove who you are**.'* (my emphasis)

Without an (apparently) authentic official document, you may not be who you say you are. Some official body or government institution needs to have agreed with your claimed identity. Without this kind of evidence, you're going to need help to find another. One alternative you may be offered is a combination of writing and witnessing – signing a document in the presence of a lawyer and then reciting a 'solemn declaration' to this person that both the name and the signature that she has sat there watching you write are yours and yours alone.

Paperwork fills key moments in our lives. In a literate society, we expect it. Important matters have to be *put on record*. Birth and death, we take it for granted, will be expressed in written words: the newborn's identity confirmed with a birth certificate; the dead remembered with words carved, printed, or tapped into keyboards.

Between our arrival and departure, countless life experiences are mixed up in less formal writing and reading activity. The use of reading and writing to record and express these experiences is an example of what is known as the 'social practice of literacy'. It is social, because it involves people relating to each other. It is a practice, because it is a cultural activity that carries meaning and value. Seeing literacy as something that goes on in this way is different from the more common view of it, as a bunch of skills to learn at school. Seeing literacy as a social practice – as we will be suggesting throughout this book – allows us to get out of a mental box and look around us. Claims of declining standards or concerns about measuring levels can be left behind. What we can observe, instead, are the manifold ways in which writing gets mixed up in speech and both are part of social processes that occur between people.

Some twenty years of research by anthropologists, linguists and educators in a variety of cultures and societies have created this shift in perspective. Instead of literacy being seen merely as the private cognitive skills of individuals, ideas have come into circulation about it as a sociable and social matter. Instead of the world, and individuals, being seen as *either* literate *or* illiterate, these offer a way of recognising subtlety and difference: a relative view. In direct challenge to the dichotomy of a 'great divide' between oral and literate, primitive and civilised, a mass of work has been published to reveal all kinds of literacy lives being lived in communities and households that had hitherto been ignored by the dominant institutions of media and education. (Gee 1990: 49–73)

Literacy as evidence

There are three posters on the wall of a launderette in the small market town where I live in South West England. It is the only launderette in town and is a family business. In their graphic design, and in their writing style, the texts show signs of being home-made, rather than having been produced in quantity by a company for its chain of branches.

The first is typeset in black Times Roman typeface, text centred on page, all in capitals, some in bold, first line underlined; 'thank you' typed in Comic Sans typeface.

PLEASE DO NOT

PUT ANYTHING ON TOP OF THE TUMBLE

DRYERS, AS IT WILL

MELT AND STICK TO THE DRYER.

OVERFILL THE WASHING

MACHINES AS OVERFILLING WILL

CAUSE THE MACHINE TO CLEAN

LESS EFFICIENTLY AND WILL

ALSO DAMAGE THE MACHINES.

YOU MUST HAVE AT LEAST A 1

INCH GAP AT THE TOP OF THE

AGITATOR BEFORE YOU PUT THE

LID DOWN.

FAILURE TO COHERE (sic) TO THESE

WARNINGS MAY RESULT IN

MACHINE REPAIR CHARGES TO

YOU THE CUSTOMER.

THANK YOU!

The second is handwritten in felt tip pen, with some words in capitals, others not:

If you

LEAVE your

Washing unattended

IT IS AT YOUR

OWN RISK!!

We are <u>NOT</u>

RESPONSIBLE!

The third, typed in black, is accompanied by line drawing of an alarmed individual, hair standing on end, eyes wide, and hands spread in shock; the first word is all in capitals; four of the remaining five begin with capitals:

CAUTION!

Floor is

Slippery

When Wet.

Each of these texts was written, very possibly, by two people: working at the wording together, deciding how to lay it out, amending mistakes, producing the final version. Behind them is a literacy practice in our culture which says: anything to do with legal rights and obligations needs to be *put in writing*. The launderette owners were, as we put it, 'protecting themselves' with these posters; so that, in the event of a customer make a complaint (about their washing being poorly washed or the dryer melting their garments or the machines breaking down or their washing being stolen or their ankle being sprained after slipping on the floor) they would be able to point to these texts as *evidence that they had warned them*. If the unhappy customer wanted to make a claim for financial compensation, this would be evidence that could be used in a court of law. So, as well as being a kindly warning against any mishap, the message of these posters is also: 'Don't bother trying to get any money from us if you don't do these things: what you are looking at says: you won't get it.'

4

The concept of written texts as *evidence* is in such common use that we barely question it. In order to qualify for state benefits, an unemployed person has to show 'evidence' of having been looking for work. It is not enough to give a spoken account of where you have been or who you have rung up. The evidence must be written. This is well illustrated by a study of people trying to get work. A team of researchers set out to discover whether people with literacy difficulties might have problems in doing so. Their main finding, from a sample of one hundred long-term unemployed people in the North of England, was that many of them could not understand why they might need better literacy skills at all, when the jobs for which they were applying had very little reading or writing involved in them. The task for which they *did* need literacy skills was that of completing the forms required by Job Centres and unemployment benefit offices. There was a further literacy demand at this stage: the requirement to provide written proof of having been actively seeking work. For people who are used to applying for white-collar jobs with major companies, as the researchers point out, this may not be a problem. As long as the person has hung on to the paperwork – photocopies of job adverts, letters of application and responses from employers – the file can be compiled without too much trouble. But for everybody else, things are more complicated. In the research sample, many had asked friends and family to look out for jobs for them, or turned up casually at workplaces on the off-chance of jobs being available. They would rarely meet a manager, let alone get interviewed or written to by one. Yet without written evidence of these activities, proof of efforts to find a job, an individual risks losing money to which they are entitled (Davies 1994).

This study also showed how much form-*reading* is required for forms to be completed: time spent in trying to understand what the form-writer might *mean* by this or that question. Another study which examined this in some detail described how an applicant-writer has to fit themselves into the 'fixed notions' that the form-designer appears to have of them. From their research into how university students filled in a government form to claim help with health costs, Marcia Fawns and Roz Ivanič give an example of this:

> Page 8 asks, "Do you have a job?" but this question cannot be addressing students because there is only a yes/no option. There is no box to tick if you do vacation work, which caused difficulties for Gary and Jay who both have holiday employment. (Fawns and Ivanič 2001: 89)

In order to answer the questions, the student applicants had to think themselves into a false either/or picture of themselves: in this case, *either* as 'workers' *or* as 'unemployed'. The exercise of filling in forms such as these, they concluded, is like 'conducting a self-analysis in terms of bureaucratically imposed categories' (*ibid.*: 90).

In workplaces themselves, the demand for record-keeping of actions taken, estimates made, products delivered, and so on, seems universal. In the public services, what has come to be known as 'the audit culture' requires that in areas such as health and education a mass of evidence be provided both of promise and delivery: forms completed about expected outcomes, other forms about achievements and evaluation. A paper trail must be made, to show how decisions were made and members of the public dealt with. Teachers, trainers, doctors, nurses, managers and administrators speak of feeling 'inundated' with paperwork. It constitutes a literacy practice on a large scale: a cultural phenomenon, with values and prices attached to it (funding depends on targets achieved, and so on). And meanwhile, the very word *audit* carries its own history, taking us back to a time when the completed forms were not written, but spoken: utterances that had to be heard.

The question of practices

The wording and typing or handwriting of the posters in the launderette, together with any discussion involved in what to say and what to omit, constituted a literacy *event*. The value given to them by their authors and their readers, linked to the cultural assumption both would share that written texts may be used as evidence in law, constitute the literacy *practice*.

In discussion about literacy events and practices, most of us find the first easier to grasp than the second. David Barton, a key writer on the topic, has made several attempts to clarify the distinction. In an early piece he wrote that literacy events are the particular activities in which literacy has a role and literacy practices are 'the general cultural ways of utilizing literacy that people draw upon in a literacy event' (Barton 1994: 5). He gave the example of a note for the milkman. Writing the note and putting it somewhere to be read, he argued, is a literacy event. The decision to do it, finding pen and paper, deciding what to write and where to leave it, all, according to Barton, 'make use of our literacy practices'.

Brian Street, another key writer in the 'New Literacy Studies' group, argued two years later for some recognition of the values, attitudes, feelings and social relationships that get mixed up in the thing. In his words:

> Literacy practices' incorporate not only 'literacy events', as empirical occasions to which literacy is integral, but also 'folk models' of those events and the ideological preconceptions that underpin them. (Street 1993: 12–13)

David Barton's subsequent 'introduction to the ecology of written language' contains a considerably developed account of the term. He suggests we might like to think about literacy practices as 'the social practices associated with the written word' (Barton 1994: 37) and offers another way to understand them:

> An alternative starting-point for a study of the social basis of literacy could be institutional practices around literacy, examining religion, capitalism,

advertising, etc as social practices. It is important to see how the state, the church and multinational corporations use literacy to plan, record, control and influence, and how people participate in these practices. (ibid.: 42)

In this construction, the warnings in the launderette would be an expression of the literacy practice of the legal system; their authors acting as participants in this institutional practice.

In their substantial study of 'reading and writing in one community', published four years later, Barton and Hamilton invert Street's image of practices and events. While he offers us a picture of *practices* which incorporate events, they suggest – more helpfully, for us I think – that the careful observation of a series of *events* allows us to infer the practices that lie behind them. As they see it, 'texts are a crucial part of literacy events, and the study of literacy is partly a study of texts and how they are produced and used'. Putting the three elements together, they produce a pleasing equation:

Literacy is best understood as a set of social practices; these can be inferred from events which are mediated by written texts.

Of the characteristics of literacy understood in this way that Barton and Hamilton then set out, they include just one that makes explicit reference to literacy practices. These, they say

... are patterned by social institutions and power relationships, and some ... become more dominant, visible and influential than others.

(Barton and Hamilton 1998:7)

For Barton and Hamilton, then, literacy practices are 'cultural ways of utilising literacy'. This is a rather more abstract view than Barton's first account of the literacy practice involved in writing a note to the milkman. Yet the concreteness of practice seems to draw them like a magnet. Each of the four case studies that follow in *Local Literacies* have the same subtitle: 'so-and-so's *literacy practices*' (Harry's, Shirley's, June's, Cliff's) and in each case, the activities described seem to constitute what Barton and Hamilton had earlier defined as *events* – the observable activities engaged in by the individuals when they were using reading and/or writing. We see Harry enjoying his ruling passion (memories of the Second World War) through using the library and writing his memoirs. We learn of Shirley contributing to the local residents' organisation by editing the newsletter. We are told about June managing her finances by keeping accounts and making lists. And we discover that Cliff writes letters and a diary, collects books, shops by reference to catalogues, and engages in pub quizzes. The reader recognises that these activities may recur. But does that mean they can be termed *literacy practices*? The puzzle remains: how might we, as adult literacy educators, enable ourselves and our learners to recognise the concept of a literacy *practice*, to be inferred from literacy events? Even to say that 'literacy practices' are:

> not only the event itself but the conceptions of the reading and writing
> process that people hold when they are engaged in the event (Street 1995:
> 133)

only helps if there is an illustration. Ellayne develops this discussion further in the
next two chapters.

Meanwhile, the illustration which we have considered so far is that of the
launderette poster. Here is another that might help. If we return to the tribute to a
dead loved one, we could say the *event* is the cluster of activity involved in
someone commissioning an inscription for the headstone from the undertaker and
the stonemason carving the words on the stone. There is social interaction
(between the bereaved and the undertaker, the undertaker and the stonemason)
and speech and text are both used. The literacy *practice* we can infer from this is
that, in the culture of the people involved, it is customary to show respect and
affection for someone who has died by causing their name and a message to be
written on a material that has some permanence (stone, brass, and so on). This
literacy practice would also include other literacy events such as: reading aloud
and singing certain texts.

As Roz Ivanič points out, such a practice is, once again, the product of a time and
a place:

> In British culture, many people consider that the appropriate response to
> another person's bereavement is to send a written card or letter of condo-
> lence. A visit would be considered intrusive, unless you are a very intimate
> friend. But in Tanzanian culture, a written condolence would be considered
> disrespectful. (Ivanič 1998: 65)

Context itself, she argues, can be understood in three ways: as physical, social and
cultural. The physical time and space in which a written text is produced by the
writer is likely to be different from that in which it is read by the reader. Writer
and reader have to take account of that in our appreciation of the other person in
the relationship. Each is in a social context, each imbued with the cultural
assumptions with which we have grown up (*ibid.*: 60–61).

In a European environment, the texts of epitaph and death certificate return us
once again to the theme of evidence. To find the names on gravestones and in
certificates of people who may in some way be connected to us is to find proof
that they existed. For the Irish poet Evan Boland, such a discovery was denied
her, and she was appalled. For her, the fact that her grandmother had died without
any written evidence that she could trace gave her a feeling that she had almost
not existed, and certainly had been forgotten. After searching high and low in the
Dublin graveyard where other records said she had been buried, she found no sign
of her. 'She had no memorial' her granddaughter felt, 'because she had no name.'
(Boland 1996: 23) It was a cruel breach of the literacy practice she expected from
the burial customs of her culture.

Drawing on Ivanič's understandings of context, then: we have so far considered how the *physical time and space* of a text's production, such as medieval Europe or twentieth century Tanzania, might relate to its *social and cultural use*. In the pictures of the four people that follow, we will glimpse the relationships involved in literacy events and practices seen through these dimensions.

Portraits

Sarah

Tricia Jones

Sarah wrote:

> *I have lived in Radstock for my whole life. I am married to Bob and we have two children. Maria is seven and Liam is five. I work part-time at the moment in an old people's home as a cook, but I really want to start my own business.*

> *That's why I'm coming to college, really. I have to do essays and maybe exams when I take qualifications for floristry which is what I want to do, so I need to improve my spelling and writing. I like gardening, cooking and making dried flowers.*

Sarah was married, with two children (aged 7 and 5). She had lived all her life in the former mining town of Radstock, Somerset. She considered herself an under-achiever and was clearly frustrated by this, because she remembered being very keen to learn. A shy child, she had tried to keep in the background at school, and still carried the stigma of being placed in a class with the 'less bright kids'. Her older sister, a former member of the group, had similar experiences. Like Sarah, she left with no qualifications but had recently enrolled on several courses in an effort to improve herself. Reflecting on this, Sarah remembered her parents not being especially concerned, recalling an instance where her mother had said 'it didn't matter for girls'.

After leaving school, she had worked as an assistant in a florist shop and enjoyed learning about the flowers, although she could never get to grips with their Latin names. Her dream was to have her own florist business. Having researched the requirements for studying floristry, she had set herself the goal of applying for a place to do an NVQ Level 2 at college. Realising that this would mean writing essays, she had joined my class. She also took short leisure courses at the local college on different aspects of floristry, regularly selected books on the subject from the library, bought a monthly gardening journal and made frequent fact-finding missions to nurseries and garden centres, all with the aim of 'not wasting any more time'. She had chosen to work on a gardening project in class and often brought in text from her monthly journal upon which we based her literacy work.

Sarah's husband bought a tabloid newspaper each weekday and brought it home at night. Sarah spoke of 'flicking through the paper' when the children were in bed, preferring the women's pages and horoscope. If an item of news caught her eye she usually asked her husband to explain it; he was, she said, 'really clever'. (Further discussion with Sarah revealed that her mother would seek clarification from her father on matters of 'politics and stuff'. Perhaps that was where she had picked up this deference to the male expert on such matters.) Sarah also read the local paper each week, particularly the jobs pages which she would scan for florist shop vacancies.

As her husband used the family car to take him to his job, she used the same bus each day to get to hers and once a week to go to college. She only needed to check the timetable posted on the bus shelter when she took the children to local events. The timetable (she told me) was clear and easy to understand.

For the weekly shop, she made a shopping list, adding to it throughout the week. She enjoyed checking out new products and ingredients for use in recipes and liked to keep a look out for any in-store offers and promotions. She purchased her monthly gardening magazine and sometimes treated herself to the supermarket's own cooking periodical, often browsing through the latest publication while she waited in line at the checkout.

Sarah's experiences incorporated many different literacies; those located in home, work, leisure and education. At home, she did most of the cooking and her literacy events focussed on reading recipes from cookery books and magazines and reading labels on tins, bottles and jars. Whilst she took responsibility for sending birthday and Christmas cards to family and friends, any formal letter writing or form filling was undertaken by her husband. When I asked her about this, Sarah said she was not sure how this had evolved but that it had become an 'unwritten rule' in the household. The fact that her father had also attended to the 'official paperwork' pointed to Street's (1993: 7) consideration of the 'ideological' model of literacy and its focus on cultural and power structures in society. If certain types of literacy are more valued – in this case the formal, more powerful literacy requirements of institutions and establishments – gendered assumptions may be implicit in their practices.

These assumptions, I realised, needed to be appreciated in understanding Sarah's learning programme. For instance, she might not consider that form-filling and completion of official and financial paperwork fell within her realm of requirement and any attempt to incorporate such activities into her classroom experience would be unsuccessful. On the other hand, any activity centred around Sarah's passion for plants and flowers had the opposite effect. She read copiously around the subject and was always eager to undertake activities which would increase her skills and understanding in this area.

Different domains of life incorporate different literacies, each with its own language or register. Some of Sarah's domains may have incorporated simpler vocabulary, but if the interest was not there, she was unlikely to absorb and apply new skills in them outside the classroom. In this respect it seems more beneficial to structure work around a learner's interest, even though the inherent technical vocabulary may be more challenging. An added advantage could be that, according to Yule, jargon associated with a particular register helps to connect those who see themselves as insiders; it enhances a sense of belonging (Yule 1996: 245).

Sarah's husband had encouraged her to attend the local drama group with him. Her involvement in this offers an insight into one of her social networks. Her experience within this group was both negative and positive (supporting Barton and Hamilton's assertion that social networks can be oppressive and disruptive as well as inspiring and uplifting (Barton & Hamilton 1998:16)). As a general volunteer, she considered herself 'a bit of a jack of all trades,' believing her lack of literacy skills placed her lower down the pecking order in terms of importance. This role often required her to prompt actors who forgot their lines, thus necessitating a familiarity with the scripts. She therefore became both expert and novice, gaining access to an otherwise 'excluded' domain through implicit participation.

While Sarah viewed her role in the drama group through a fairly negative framework, she had no such qualms where her interest in gardening was concerned. While still a novice, she felt that this was learning all the time. The experience had become a positive one, focused as it was on her goals and aspirations for the future.

John

Chris Topham

John is a 62-year-old man who had lived all his life in London until coming to Swindon with his wife, nine months before we met. Following a period of ill-health, he had been unemployed for some time and came to Third Age Challenge, where I work, on the recommendation of an adviser at the Job Centre. In the course of his initial interview he confided that he could not write and so I was asked to work with him.

John said he was very embarrassed by his inability to spell and by his poor handwriting which members of his family said looked 'like a 5-year-old's'. He wanted to learn to write so that he could write letters to the Council about issues that concern him. He also wanted to be able to fill in forms and deal with official correspondence.

A 'war baby', John had suffered ill health from an early age, missing a lot of schooling, especially between the ages of eight and ten, due to bronchitis and asthma. He was sent away from home to a boarding school/convalescent home in Hampshire for a year. On his return he was sent to a special school, known locally as the 'backward' school, about which he still felt very embarrassed. Although the pupils were taught in small classes and some of the teachers were good he left school at 15 unable to read or write properly.

Until his recent ill-health John had always been employed, working in engineering machine shops, in factories, as a driver and as a cleaner. His strategies for dealing with writing tasks included taking mileage sheets home to complete. Since having a heart attack and moving to Swindon he had found it impossible to get suitable part-time work. He believed his age and health counted against him.

About ten years before, John had made up his mind to learn to read. Having enrolled at an evening class, he found that the tutor was one of his former teachers at the 'special school'. This tutor was very encouraging and supportive and the lessons were a success. John told me that he now felt able to read well enough to meet his needs and had decided the time was right to do something about his writing.

When he first came to a basic skills class, he could only write his name in block capitals or as a 'signature' which consisted of his initials and a squiggle. He could not reliably spell his real first name correctly. We mostly worked around spelling and practising cursive handwriting. Not long before we met, he had done a short piece of independent writing for the first time and became quite emotional. He seemed to swing between being proud of his achievements and frustrated with his difficulties. My own observations led me to wonder whether he might be dyslexic and my sense was that if he knew that some of his difficulty could be accounted for in this way, it might have improved his self-esteem.

When he was living in London, John's networks would have been denser than they were when we met, having been comprised of family, friends, neighbours and workmates. It appeared that some other members of his family had literacy problems as well as himself (his mother did not read or write and one of his brothers had similar difficulties to his own but without the same health problems). In these circumstances it is understandable that reading did not, apparently, play much part in family life. It also follows that they kept in touch by telephone.

Being unemployed, John did not have regular contact with workmates, and although he met other people at a weekly swimming group there was apparently little time for conversation there. However, he spoke of developing new networks in Swindon among his immediate neighbours and in the town as a whole. He had enquired about being a voluntary Ranger in one of the town's parks and had signed up to join a group of Council residents to discuss matters of local interest. Both of these new ventures brought him into contact with a wider range of people. Joining a Basic Skills class seemed to be another way of doing the same.

John spoke with a London accent, of which he was proud. It had given rise to some lively 'banter' (his own word) and on one occasion to his being called a 'Cockney . . .'. He was interested in the variety of West Country accents he had come across but did not speak of any misunderstanding through dialect difference. We had been meeting at Third Age Challenge on a fairly regular basis for four months and I had become a part of his social network. When we talked, it was difficult to tell whether he made any adjustments to the way he spoke. Unless he was recounting another person's speech or mimicking a more 'elevated' style, he used Standard English grammar. His conversations with others in the office were similar. He believed that people should talk 'properly' and said that he 'corrected' himself if he spoke 'sloppily' but he did not consciously speak in a different way according to the person or group he is talking to. He was, however, well aware that he needed to use a formal style when writing formal letters.

John's local neighbourhood was a residential estate in Swindon, and the town centre. In his neighbourhood he used the library, a community centre and a branch office of BBC Radio Swindon. He liked to call in there for a chat as he could discuss local issues without writing letters. In the town centre he visited the council offices and the Job Centre as well as Third Age Challenge centre where I worked. Wherever he went, John would read notices and pick up leaflets which interested him. This is how he learned about the Volunteer Ranger scheme mentioned earlier.

Many of the literacy events in John's day-today life were related to official bodies and organisations. His fortnightly visits to the Job Centre involved completing and signing forms, and reading job details. He was also in regular contact with the Borough Council, in person or by phone or in received correspondence with them. In the post he also got bills and details of medical appointments. On various occasions he quoted or read to me from these letters. Although he sometimes stumbled over unusually long words, he seemed to have no real difficulty understanding 'officialese'. However, when he was sent a briefing paper for a meeting he gave up and relied on the explanation given at the meeting itself. His comment on it was that it was written in 'lawyers' language'.

There was a substantial difference between John's reading and writing levels. He could read most of what he needed to but could write very little. When the local paper had run a series of articles about vandalism, he had felt very strongly about the issue and rung their offices to tell them what he thought. He said they were very interested but asked him to put his opinions in writing. John uses the telephone and face-to-face conversations well, but the written word still holds great power.

On a recent job application, John listed reading as one of his hobbies. He regularly read *The Sun* and the local paper. He liked to tell me what he was reading but did not bring in any articles to discuss even though I encouraged him to do so. He also used a TV listings guide. He used his local library to browse in the gardening books and to find information. He once asked the librarian to help him find the 'To be or not to be ...' speech from Hamlet so that he could read it himself. He enjoyed looking in the *Dictionary of Quotations* and memorised some passages for pleasure.

On his visits to the Jobcentre he was expected to look at details of jobs but he preferred to go directly to see an adviser. (Perhaps this is because he had not developed the skills of skimming and scanning.) He would then be given details of jobs for which he should apply. These were often inappropriate for reasons of health and sometimes for other reasons. On one occasion he was told to apply for a job as a car park attendant and when he looked at the requirements closely the employer was asking for the equivalent of GCSE English and Maths Grades A–C. This posed a whole host of questions about literacy and employment, not least: how carefully had the advisers read job details?

It seemed there was very little informal literacy in John's life. Any writing he did feel he needed to do was formal. Occasionally he would leave notes for his wife to say where he had gone. Other than that, he did not have any practice in writing notes, greeting cards, lists and so on; his wife wrote all these. She also wrote any letters and helped John with forms. In short, it appeared that John was quite happy to leave the literacy in the vernacular domain of his life in her hands. He did not see writing family letters as important. What primarily concerned him was the literacy of the wider society in which he lived. He wanted access to the dominant literacy practices supported by powerful institutions. Having perceived himself as an outsider, he saw improving his literacy skills as a means of achieving his personal goals. A side effect might also have been to win him greater respect from his family and friends when they saw what he could do outside the home.

John's experience of reading for pleasure was still in its infancy. The search for the speech from Shakespeare seems to have been prompted partly by his wanting to prove to himself that he could read culturally important texts and partly from a sense he had that there was a different world of poetry and ideas that he could tap into and share in, and which excited him.

Throughout his life, John had been conscious of the power of literacy and consequently perceived himself as relatively powerless. Once he became proficient at writing, he hoped to show his family that he could be independent and should be treated with greater respect – among his neighbourhood and society at large – to contribute his ideas and opinions and share in the power of the institutions with which he is connected. As a result of his own learning and his openness to change, John's literacy life was changing. I admired him for the insight which had led him to focus on writing as a means to achieving his personal goals and for his willingness to work at acquiring a new skill at this stage in his life. I also thought it was wonderful to see him take pleasure in reading.

Marie Anne

Kauser McCallum

Marie Anne, 43 years old, was born in Kent. At the age of 13 she had moved to Nottingham with her family, and two years later, to Swindon, where, at the time of this study, she was living with her husband James and her son Carl. As a small child, she had lost the sight of one eye and spent her childhood in and out of hospitals having operations to save the other. At the primary school, she recalled being bullied; her parents moved her to a convent school, but there, the problems she had with her English and maths were not picked up.

As an adult, Marie Anne had undertaken a range of voluntary jobs, mainly in the area of care or in hospital work. She expressed a real passion for history, reading biographies, watching historic films – *Titanic* being her favourite – and making regular visits to museums with her son. This is how she described her changing literacy ambitions in the pen sketch she wrote for me:

> *I came to a Basic Skills class because my Maths was horrible to witness. I had hiding methods to cover my errors, and a very heavy purse of £1 coins.*

> *My English is better but writing a formal Letter or a CV for a job was a horrible nightmare.*

> *[Since coming here] I have passed Level one in English. CLAIT 1 for computers and Numberpower Entry Level in Maths and I write to my pen friends abroad in Canada, Russia, school friends in England and E-mail to my cousin abroad.*

> *I would like to understand words in novels, complete forms, have a job I like and enjoy and have qualifications in English and maths.*

At the time we met, Marie Anne had been attending Basic Skills classes for over three years; as we talked about literacy events and practices in her life, she often reflected back to the time when she had lacked many of the skills she now possessed. We discussed the literacy activities that were involved for her at work, in the home and for leisure.

Quite recently, Marie Anne had joined the Great Western Hospital's team of volunteers who help to feed patients. She said she had applied unsuccessfully for this position a few years ago before. She believed that she was rejected then because she had not been able to fill out the application form properly and that the reason she had been successful the second time was that the interviewer had asked her questions and then entered her answers on a computer. My discussion with her indicated that the form required applicants to provide information about previous work experience, reasons for applying to become a volunteer and the names of two referees. In addition they were asked to fill in a medical form. This listed illnesses and disorders with many of which, she told me, she was not familiar.

As a new volunteer, Marie Anne had to complete a two and a half days training programme. This entailed a number of tasks each of which we listed. These, regrouped, seem to provide a picture of three separate literacy events, in each of which speaking and listening mixed with writing and reading:

1. Enrolling on the course:

    ● Sign the course register;

    ● Read and complete three different forms (to get a security pass, to get photographs for this and to be reimbursed for her travel costs);

    ● Read and understand signs about injections (such as hepatitis B, a requirement for all volunteers before starting work on the wards).

2. Absorbing new information:

    ● Listen to talks on hygiene, healthy diet, speech therapy, fire drill etc.

    ● Participate in group discussions on course topics;

    ● Skim-read a lot of handouts;

    ● Participate in games and role-plays on how to assist patients.

3. Have her learning assessed:

    ● Complete quizzes and questionnaires to show her understanding.

I had been wondering how she would have coped with some of these and at our second meeting, we discussed this. Marie Anne explained that a trainee nurse had been working with her who had explained any difficult words and spent time with her to clarify the handouts.

At the end of her training, Marie Anne was assigned to a ward. On each visit she had to: sign in, follow written procedures for washing hands; talk to the patients and feed them; fill in a chart for each patient to show what s/he ate; and help the patients fill in the menu card for the next day. Most of this work she had found straightforward and within her capabilities; but she had had difficulty reading and understanding the specialist terminology. (For example, she was still not sure of the difference between clinical and manual handling.) We talked about the implications of this for her and the hospital. The reason she felt it was not a great problem was that there were (as at the training course) auxiliary nurses on hand who could provide support and guidance.

In contrast with this, looking through a leaflet produced by the hospital 'Finding your way to and around The Great Western Hospital,' I was struck by how many other medical terms Marie Anne could read and explain (such as ENT/ Audiology, Rehabilitation and Therapies, Urology and Radiology). The answer lay in her life experience. She recalled them, she said, partly from her contact with hospitals as a child and partly from the work she later did for several years in a care home.

At home, her husband James was responsible for paying the bills and dealing with paperwork when they took on new ventures like opening an account. She had never been comfortable with figures, the small print still worried her and she said she was happy to let him tackle these tasks, as any mistake on her part might have consequences for their family finances. However, she said she now had the confidence to open the 'official looking letters' they received and would ring up her husband if a letter seemed to need an urgent response. She and James would go shopping together for any large items for the house; she would sort out delivery details over the phone; but she felt she needed help completing orders. She did not, however, go shopping on her own (except to buy small items like an onion or a pint of milk from the shop nearby) as she was petrified of dealing with money.

Marie Anne had recently joined a reading group at Swindon Library. She hoped that this would encourage her to read a wider genre of books and discuss them with other members of the group. A few years before, she told me, the idea of doing this would have been unthinkable.

Since joining basic skills classes she had gained the confidence to participate in a training programme for work and expand her leisure activities. She could now, for example, read maps, which she said she had not been able to do before joining a class. However, she still needed more confidence in tackling any other texts which involved mathematical systems, such as recipes.

After our first meeting I was intrigued by Marie Anne's descriptions of her literacy practices. She had told me that she regularly wrote long and newsy letters to her pen friends; yet in the class she had considerable difficulty composing informal letters. She often lacked the ability to organise her thoughts in a structured and coherent manner on paper; yet her summaries of the Hodder and Stoughton books (abridged for Basic Skills students) had been succinct and well composed within the structure of a single paragraph. I began to wonder whether she may be describing the person she wanted to be and the skills to which she aspired rather than those she actually possessed. I decided to explore these points at our second meeting.

When we met again, I shared my confusion with her. I soon learned that she had a very tight and supportive network, which encouraged her to expand her range of domains. This network included her husband, son, and her friend, Debbie, her mother and her school friend Diane. Marie Anne carried a mobile phone, so she could seek advice from within this network whenever she was in an uncomfortable situation. In addition, the tutors at Swindon College and her colleagues at work represented a wider network upon which she could, and did draw.

It was her husband, Marie Anne told me, who had encouraged her to join a WEA course to improve her maths. Her childhood friend, Diane, who lived in Kent, had suggested that she improved her writing skills by communicating with pen friends. To ensure that the pen friends receive 'error free' letters, they had devised an efficient method. Marie Anne would first write a letter to Diane; they then discussed her letter over the phone to make corrections; then Marie Anne would rewrite the letter and post it.

Perhaps the major problem Marie Anne faced was in transferring the skills she had developed in one domain so that she was able to apply them in others. For example, although she had no difficulty in reading coach and bus timetables, she was frustrated in trying to do the same with an airline timetable, because the former were expressed on the basis of the twelve hour clock and the latter, on the twenty-four hour clock. Again, while she was not intimidated by certain long and technical words within a medical context, she could get stuck on those in simpler texts. And surprisingly, she told me she felt alienated by texts which combined illustration and text, or diagrammatic presentations of information. Given that such means of presentation are usually used in order to make the information contained more accessible, this struck me as ironic.

In the process of doing this study, I realised that Marie Anne's perception of a literate and numerate person was based on very traditional uses of literacy: the ability to read novels and to compose formal letters. She disregarded the value of more everyday literacy practices which she dealt with in other contexts, which she could cope with.

What Marie Anne wanted was access to the higher status kinds of literacy: the library reading group; the literacy of paid employment.

Dave

Sarah Lyster

The autonomous model of literacy, described by Brian Street (1993: 5–7), is viewed almost as a science of technical terms and quite separate from any social context. I may previously have shared this view, but since working with people such as Dave and trying to enable them to improve their literacy skills, I no longer do. The ideological model, which Brian Street proposes, seems to me to be more relevant to my understanding of a student like Dave. The literacy needs of each individual are unique; as teachers, we should aim to meet these within their own social context.

This, then, was Dave's context, as he represented it to me. Aged 31, he lived alone in a small modern house. He had a brother who was very successful in business and married with children. Dave was not jealous of him, he told me, but would love to have a wife and children because it would keep his parents happy. He kept the views of his mother in mind always, whether because she would be pleased or because she would disapprove and therefore must be prevented from finding out about something.

Dave had two main hobbies: line dancing and trucks. He attended a line dancing class each week, always arriving early to help set the room up. His interest in trucks developed from a childhood fascination for cars; he regularly watched banger racing and went to shows like 'Truckfest'. He also built models from plastic kits and had numerous examples in his house.

He had left school at 15 to train to become a mechanic. This involved him coming to college for one day each week, but after two years he was made redundant. He then started work for Tesco, joining the fresh produce team. He had great difficulty reading the labels and so was moved to the 'back door' where the goods were delivered. This highlighted his problems; he was unable to write the notes and read the documents before signing them and was quickly moved to trolleys – with a wage cut. His manager arranged for him to have an interview at the college to start basic skills literacy classes.

In class, Dave said that he was very keen to learn how to write 'in joined up'. I asked whether he had learned joined writing at school and why he wanted to learn now. He replied that there were two teachers who persistently told him his joined writing was illegible and so he had changed to writing in capital letters or print. He felt that he would like to learn now as he thought his college work would look neater.

I wondered what effect these teachers had had on his learning; they had certainly played a part in damaging his self-esteem. I was surprised because the graphic style Dave had adopted was very legible, as I saw when I asked him to write his name on a piece of paper and he did, linking all the letters. I asked whether his signature was different, but he signed his name in exactly the same way. The signature was completely legible and we talked about that. He believed that was because he had written his signature many times and because it was easy to read he did not have to write his name out again. Dave found it amusing that with many people their signature is illegible and simply a way in which they mark a paper, which is the same each time they make the mark. He found it worrying that a signature might need the person's name written again at the side. The prospect of having to write the same thing twice in the same place worried him.

Even in today's technological world, as Jane Mace has noted, the signature 'continues to be a literacy practice which has a deeply symbolic importance as a tool for empowerment' (2001: 45). This was certainly true for Dave, who had to sign his work sheets in order to get paid, but until quite recently this had been the only writing he did, apart from at his weekly literacy class. He never wrote lists; he had a very good memory and if he needed to make important decisions or sign important forms where he may have had to write, his mother accompanied him. These activities were rare and recent. He had bought a house a year before. With help from his mother, he had set up systems to pay all his bills by direct debit. He managed some forms himself but liked to have her there as reassurance. Having been bullied in his early life, he was very wary of strangers who might try to take advantage. Overall, he avoided writing wherever possible: this included his signature.

When Dave wrote a paragraph about his weekend (which had involved banger racing) he produced a text which, though it contained several spelling mistakes, was quite understandable. He worried that some of the joins he had made between letters were not exactly as I had shown him. I had to explain that we each develop a style of writing to suit us and that, although similar, the style of writing is personal and unique to each individual. This work gave him a new sense of success and he was evidently pleased.

Dave knew a great deal about trucks, from their fuel consumption and their colours, to their tyre sizes and wheel numbers. How had he become so knowledgeable about them? He told me he bought a truck magazine, which he would analyse, taking special interest in all the technical specifications. He said that it was too hard to read but he bought it for the pictures. He always used images first and only went on to look at the written text if he needed clarification.

For many years Dave had been making model trucks and cars from plastic kits. His grandfather had helped him when he was a child, but he was now very competent and able to tackle large and complex kits. These kits had mostly diagrams to follow, with short passages of text describing safety issues and a list of accessories required, such as glue and paint. Some of these models were made in Korea and the instructions were written in poorly translated English. Only the safety instructions were written; diagrams described the assembly. Safety instruction 3 is a good example: 'BE CAREFUL TO USE TOOLS AND KNIVES AS THESE CAN CAUSE INJURY'. It goes on to advise care with the adhesive: 'DO NOT PUT INTO MOUTH OR EYE. IF MISTAKENLY PUT INTO, WASH OUT PROMPTLY WITH FULL WATER AND CONSULT A DOCTOR IMMEDIATELY'. Fortunately both these instructions could be regarded as good sense, rather than specialist information. I do not know whether Dave read them or not.

The magazines provided a useful reference for model building; the box itself usually gave inadequate information as to colours and transfers.

Dave's other literacy ambition was to read Michael Palin's *Sahara*. His grandfather and uncle had given him this book as a Christmas present. They had thought he would enjoy reading it as he had enjoyed the television series and the book contained many photographs. The text is quite complicated and at first he had struggled with it. He and I read three chapters together; from this, he learnt how to read the familiar words and make a good guess at others, using phonics to decode those he didn't know, but making a note of them as he went along. He would then look up each word in a dictionary and reread for understanding the sentence which contained the word.

By this time, Dave read relatively well. The words he found difficult were the complex ones, which confuse many people. He had developed the skill of using the pictures alongside the text to help him work out meaning. This was evidently a strategy that he had been using for years. It could explain why he would not even attempt to read a book without pictures, not even an article in a magazine. Equally, he would make an attempt to read any text which had pictures, even if the lexis was extremely complex. From the Internet, which had become a new source of truck information, especially pictures, he would download and print a mass of material. Once again, faced with a limited amount of text accompanied by pictures, he was not daunted by the information.

Dave liked to talk about his interests and would engage in conversation about any topic. In June 2003 he was interviewed live on the local radio station about organic fruit and vegetables and was on air for ten minutes. (The programme had been advertised; Dave had rung up and had then been selected for interview.) He taped the interview and made copies for his parents, grandparents and his boss. He was evidently very proud of his achievement.

Dave loved information and remembered things he felt might be useful; he was a good questioner. At the same time, he worried about failure and so would limit the amount of writing he undertook, except at college – where he seemed to feel confident to try and pleased to learn. College was an important part of his life; he had few friends and his tutor was someone independent whom he could trust to help him.

Commentary

Sarah's literacy activities included both the focused and the casual: on the one hand, the reading to support her interest in floristry, in the form of college courses, library book choices, magazine reading and visits to garden centres and nurseries.; on the other, 'flicking through' magazines after the children had gone to bed, or at supermarket checkouts.

Of particular interest is the contrast between the value she attaches to the literacy practices of her gardening interests and that which she gave to her role in the drama group she belonged to. In both, she has a sense of herself as a novice. But while the learning she is doing in gardening and floristry is driven by a sense of her aspiration to achieve status in that field, as a member of the drama group she seems less concerned about achievement, choosing the role of prompt, rather than that of actor. In terms of literacy practices, this is a deceptively low-key choice. Though she may be hidden in the wings, outside the glare of the spotlight, the person with the prompt sheet has her own part to play: a key actor in the task of breathing life into the script.

Referring to her husband for the political and formal literacy practices in their lives, she herself takes responsibility for the literacy events necessary for the family shopping and cooking: as Tricia Jones suggests, a familiarly gendered division of literacy labour.

In John's literacy life, there is the theme of change. Having made up his mind to learn to read some years before, he had gained sufficient confidence to deal with what he needed to as a reader. For him, writing was the issue now: in particular, his handwriting, and his spelling. In this account he comes across as a man who has no great trouble in socialising; he is a 'great talker', who calls in to the offices of the local radio station 'for a chat', rings up the local newspaper when he finds something he feels strongly about, uses the library, community centre, swimming pool, and attends meetings about local affairs. As Chris Topham puts it, he wanted to be the kind of writer who could operate confidently among 'dominant literacy practices'. He browses freely through papers, magazines and books, reads notices 'wherever he goes' and picks up leaflets that interest him. But what he is looking for seems to be the dignity that he would feel if he could deal independently with the literacy practices of employment. He has changed; he wants to change some more. Recalling Paul Davies' study, we can remember that the kind of writer that John seeks to become entails a certain sophistication as a reader, too.

Like Sarah, Marie Anne had to deal in her work with technical language that was not just Latinate, but Latin. While for Sarah this meant dealing with the botanical names for plants and flowers, for Marie Anne, it entailed medical conditions and their remedies.

For Marie Anne, the status she found in the literacy of novel-reading and formal letter-writing eclipsed any value that may be found in the literacy she could already do. There is, too, an interesting contrast between her account of herself writing copious letters to her pen friends in her home domain; yet in the setting of the classroom, seeming to find trouble in composing informal letters. Could this be the sense she had of (very literally) 'not feeling at home' in the latter? Or had it something to do with the authenticity of the first activity and the artificiality of a classroom task with a reader who both does not exist yet is also very present – in the person of the teacher/assessor?

The example of literacy events that occurred for her in her work as a hospital volunteer enable us to envisage spoken and written language alternating with each other, and recognise the official nature of the texts that had to be produced. Although by their nature confidential, medical records have a public status: they belong to the institution, not the author; they may be used as evidence (that word again) in the event of any litigation by a patient.

Marie Anne may not have liked pictures in her text; for Dave, the last of this series of portraits, they were essential. For his model-building, diagrams provided more reliable instructions than the written text. To pursue his interest in trucks, he studied the pictures in magazines and on the net, only resorting to the written word if these were not clear. This is a man with a concern for the look of things, who minded when the handwritten script he produced did not tally with the loops and joins of the model provided by his teacher. For him, his choice of reading is a book which follows his viewing of its film version on television. Unlike Marie Anne, he seemed to find the college environment liberated him from the worries he had had about writing, and the social context of the class enabled him to take risks that he would not take elsewhere. The challenge for him, as for her, was how to take his sense of confidence as a reader and writer in one context into other, less comfortable ones.

Chapter 2

Social networks

Ellayne Fowler

In this chapter we trace a theoretical path from the language use of the individual to the literacy practices of a group. The case studies which follow illustrate the importance of social networks in learners' lives, literacy practices and learning. We begin by focusing on language variation and how this can be explained in terms of individuals and then in terms of the communities they belong to. The introduction of practice theory and a wider view of language interaction lead us to literacy practices. Five teachers then provide us with an illustration of this view through the portraits they have created with their learners.

The individual and language

Our use of language and literacy signals our membership of the social groups we belong to and move in and out of in our lives. When we hear someone speak we can generally tell their gender and age from their speech. We may well know something about their social class and/or ethnic origin and/or the region they come from. Social factors such as gender, age, ethnicity, social class and region are encompassed in elements of pronunciation, tone, pitch, vocabulary and grammar. A combination of these social factors has a great influence on our idiolect, that is, the very individual cast of our speech.

However, we don't speak in the same way in all contexts. Sociolinguists explain these linguistic choices in terms of

- Participants (who is speaking and listening?)

- Setting (where is the conversation happening?)

- Topic (what is it about?)

- Function (why is the conversation taking place?)

We can adapt our speech or literacy practices according to a combination of these factors. Let's take the fictional example of Mary who buys a pair of high-heeled shoes. The first time she wears them the heel breaks off, so Mary takes them back to the shop, but after a heated discussion with the assistant she is unable to get a refund. Mary's report of this incident could take a variety of linguistic expression, according to participants, setting, topic and function.

Participants	Mary and her friend, Elsie	Mary and a Citizen's Advice Bureau worker	Mary and the shop manager
Setting	Café	Citizen's Advice Bureau	Letter[1]
Topic	The broken shoes	The broken shoes	The broken shoes
Function	Telling a story and sharing experiences	Explaining what happened and seeking advice	To complain and ask for compensation
Language variety/style	Animated and supportive conversation. Informal language and use of slang	Formal conversation. Mary avoids slang. Mostly questions and answers	Formal letter using formal English.

This is a short example, but it allows us to focus on the different ways we use language in different situations. However, an important point to highlight in this example is that I have taken for granted that Mary has access to a wide linguistic repertoire. Janet Holmes usefully defines a linguistic repertoire in terms of community; 'In any community the distinguishable varieties (or codes) which are available for use in different social contexts form a kind of repertoire of available options' (Holmes 2001: 7). This takes the focus away from the individual and to the community as a source of linguistic choice.

Research in sociolinguistics has shown how membership of groups and our social networks have a more profound effect on our language than the social factors outlined above. Mary's linguistic repertoire is not simply about having skills, but includes her awareness of and access to a range of language and literacy practices. It may be, for example, that in Mary's community, people would get redress for a complaint by complaining in person to the shop manager, having taken advice from other members of the community in an informal way through discussion outside their local shop. In this case, Mary may have the skills to write the letter in terms of vocabulary and spelling, but writing a letter of complaint would not be her own preferred option. In order to explore these social aspects of language the concept of social networks is useful.

---

[1]   Written text has to create its own context to be able to stand alone, which is why the letter is its own setting.

Social networks

Sociolinguistic studies that attempt to capture and explain language change and variety have explored ways of describing how an individual uses language that go beyond finite groupings such as gender, age and ethnicity. One way that sociolinguists looked at the language of groups of people is Labov's concept of a 'speech community'. This is, he says, 'best defined as a group who share the same norms in regard to language. In this sense, older and younger speakers in New York City belong to slightly different speech communities' (Labov 1972:158). What people in a speech community share are the values they place on certain linguistic forms, such as the dropping of initial 'h's.

The work of James and Lesley Milroy in Belfast built on this concept of community, that is, a cohesive group to which people know they belong. Lesley Milroy in particular shows how patterns of linguistic variation are governed far more by people's social networks within their community than other social factors. A social network is made up of the people you know and the relationships between them. Two useful concepts for discussing social networks are *plexity* and *density*: concepts which are illustrated by some of the pieces later in this chapter.

Density is a measure of whether people in a social network know each other. Think about your own social network and consider whether your friends know each other independently of their relationship with you. If they do it is a *dense network*.

Plexity is a measurement of the types of relationships within a social network. Again think about your own social network and ask yourself whether your interactions with people take place in one context or in a number of contexts. The first constitutes a *uniplex* relationship and the second a *multiplex* one. If you know your neighbour only as a neighbour, then you are in a uniplex relationship with each other. If you and she also work together or belong to the same darts team, your relationship is a multiplex one.

In her study in Belfast, Lesley Milroy found that different types of social networks either inhibit or encourage linguistic change or variation. Men in Ballymacarett, for example, who worked in the local shipyard and had dense networks, were less likely to countenance linguistic change, than women in the same district, who travelled outside the area for work and were less disposed to resist linguistic change. The fact that the women were more likely to have a wide linguistic repertoire was not simply attributable to gender, as these findings were reversed in Clonard, where women stayed in dense networks in the local area and men travelled outside for work.

We can relate these findings to the research of Arlene Fingeret who looked at the social networks of illiterate adults and uncovered 'social networks that are characterized by reciprocal exchange' (Fingeret 1983:134): that is, while non-readers went to readers in the network for help, they brought other skills to the network that were as highly or more highly valued. Further to this though, Fingeret suggests that these social networks can be classified in two ways, as either *local* or *cosmopolitan*, although she posits this as a continuum rather than two discrete options. Basically, non-reading adults with a cosmopolitan social network were 'deeply involved in literate society' (*ibid.*:138); that is, they mixed and interacted with people with a range of educational backgrounds outside of their local geographical area. On the other hand, those with a local network were less geographically mobile, 'which reinforces close-knit networks in which all the members know each other' (*ibid.*:139). In terms of language the *local* illiterate adult would be more resistant to linguistic change and in terms of literacy they would have much less exposure to and understanding of a wide range of literacy practices.

How then does this impact on our understanding of how literacy students use language? A student who comes from a dense, multiplex social network may well have difficulties building a linguistic repertoire outside of that speech community, through lack of practice or exposure. In this chapter, Mandy Weatheritt's account of the social network of Moze shows a mostly uniplex one (most interactions take place in one context, such as work or socialising) which lacks density (few of the people in the network know or have relationships with each other outside of their relationship with Moze). What becomes clear in this and other examples is that the literacy group and teacher become part of the social network of the learner.

Although social networks have proved a useful way of looking at linguistic variation at the level of the group, rather than the individual, they do focus on language and linguistic variables, such as 'h' dropping and the use of 'in' instead of 'ing'. More recent inter-disciplinary research has moved on to the idea of 'communities of practice', which allows us to consider language and literacy as fully social practices.

Recent research in social theory into the concept of community has attempted to define what we mean by it. Sometimes it can be essentially about location, as demonstrated particularly by working class communities in Milroy's study in Belfast. Other research though has focused on social networks as groups to which we feel we belong and give us a sense of community. What links those social networks are shared norms and habits. This is not to say everyone has the same habits, but that they share values. Discussions of social networks tend to highlight linked qualities of tolerance, reciprocity and trust.

Further, when we talk about literacy practices, we are taking a practice theory view of the social world, of which a prominent exponent is the sociologist and anthropologist Pierre Bourdieu. While clearly stating that you cannot strip the language away from other symbolic elements, this view acknowledges its often central role:

> Not only are linguistic features never clearly separated from the speaker's whole set of social properties (bodily hexis[2], physiognomy, cosmetics, clothing), but phonological (or lexical, or any other) features are never clearly separated from other levels of language, and the judgement which classifies a speech form as "popular" or a person as "vulgar" is based, like all practical predication, on sets of indices which never impinge on consciousness in that form. (Bourdieu 1991: 89).

So we classify people, not just by what they say but how they say it, how they look and how they act.

Communities of practice

Social networks, then, can have a more linguistic focus, as in Milroy's study, or a wider concept in terms of community. A more useful concept that has been used in recent years has been that of a 'community of practice'. This concept has arisen in the field of educational theory in the work particularly of Jean Lave and Etienne Wenger. Here the community is defined by shared practice. As Wenger writes:

> We all belong to communities of practice. At home, at work, at school, in our hobbies – we belong to several communities of practice at any given time. And the communities of practice to which we belong change over the course of our lives. (Wenger 1998: 6)

Geraldine Castleton's study of the role of literacy in the lives of homeless people in Australia highlights the importance of communities of practice in their lives. One of the roles that she highlights in the community is that of literacy broker, that is, 'someone who applies his or her literacy skills on behalf of others' (Castleton 2001: 65). As in Fingeret's work, Castleton found that:

> Such communities are characterised by the mutual exchange of skills and practices, and reflect the ways in which people in various contexts take up their roles as particular kinds of citizens (ibid.: 66)

She goes on to argue that this view of literacy requires that, 'literacy and literacy provision should focus more on the notion of *change* rather than *access*'. This, in turn, would allow providers to focus on where learners start from, what contributions they already make in networks: an emphasis on what they have, 'rather than on what they lack' (*ibid.*).

---

[2]   Bucholtz defines hexis as 'the individual's habitual and socially meaningful embodied stances and gestures, and through other aspects of physical self-presentation' (2003: 142).

Language

Penelope Eckert and Mary Bucholtz demonstrated how involvement in particular communities of practice allowed teenagers to construct their social identity. Eckert used the concept to describe groups in an American high school (which she named *burnouts* and *jocks*) and their linguistic and non-linguistic behaviour. In her chapter on high school nerds, Mary Bucholtz sets out how such communities arise:

> In communities of practice, unlike speech communities, the boundaries are determined not externally by linguists, but internally through ethnographically specific social meanings of language use. (Bucholtz 2003: 149)

Seen in these terms, language then becomes an element of social practice and the focus becomes more on research **with** rather than research **on** people.

Roles and identities

In their study of the literacy practices of a working class community in Lancaster, David Barton and Mary Hamilton used the concept of networks to focus on social groups. 'Within such networks' they report, 'people take on specific roles and assert different identities as they participate in different literacy events' (Barton and Hamilton 1998: 16). Like Fingeret, they found that 'much of people's reading and writing involved other people and was located in reciprocal networks of exchange' (*ibid.*: 254). They found, too, that personal networks were particularly important when confronting official literacy; and they note that:

> usually when people identify problems, they have networks of support and know where they can turn to for support. Alternatively, since these networks are effective, problems do not arise or are not recognised (ibid.: 161)

In an earlier paper, Barton and Padmore noted that when people talked about writing:

> it was often in terms of roles; they referred to themselves as parents, relatives, workers, neighbours, friends – each role making differing literacy demands upon them (Barton and Padmore 1994: 213)

There were clear role differences in terms of gender and roles changed over time. As we will see in the portraits that follow in this chapter, change in people's roles sometimes results from their increased confidence in their own literacy.

As Sarah's story in the previous chapter illustrated, networks can sometimes be less than supportive. In this one we will see how Ruth, who felt her family to be supportive, did not feel the same about her church. This raises again the issue, as with the high school groups, of how we create a social identity or identities within our social networks. Networks can break down and change. Like the roles we play in them, they are not static.

Education

The concepts of social network and community of practice can help us explore more fully the role and value of different literacy practices in our learners' lives. If we come back to the concept of community of practice as it was first articulated, insights for educators may be found in that bigger picture.

In *Situated Learning: Legitimate Peripheral Participation* Jean Lave and Etienne Wenger view learning as an aspect of all social activity: something we all do all the time in the real world, not merely in a classroom. Wenger takes up this theory of learning as social participation in *Communities of Practice: Learning, Meaning and Identity*. As a development of the ideas of literacy practices discussed in the previous chapter it is useful here to note Wenger's definition of **practice** itself: the concept, he says:

> connotes doing, but not just doing in and of itself. It is doing in a historical and social context that gives structure and meaning to what we do. In this sense, practice is always social practice. Such a concept of practice includes both the explicit and the tacit. (Wenger 1998: 47)

If we examine a community of practice to which we all belong at some point, that of a family, we can see how this works. The example comes from my own history. This is a brief recollection of Sunday dinner in the early 1960s in the family in which I grew up. The roles we took on – cook, table layer, washer up and so on – changed as the children got older.

When I was young we used to have a roast dinner every Sunday after listening to the radio. We listened to 'Two Way Family Favourites' and then a comedy, such as 'The Navy Lark'. Dinner (not lunch) was always roast meat and potatoes, vegetables and gravy. Pudding (not dessert) was often a fruit pie or crumble with custard. We all sat at the table to eat this meal together. Children had pop to drink and my mother and father had beer and stout respectively. We walked with dad to the Off Licence in the morning to collect the drinks. You couldn't get down from the table without asking permission. This was a special meal in the week, because we were all together – Dad worked shifts. It was also special because it was bigger and better than other meals during the week.

This illustration offers a way of accessing what a community of practice is. (It may help if you try to describe a similar event in a community of practice that you belong to.) It can take some time to tease out all the elements; for example, I haven't gone into the washing up rituals and the hierarchy of age and gender involved in these. It takes time to analyse because these practices are often implicit and not made explicit. When my youngest brother was born we didn't sit him down and explain what was involved in Sunday Dinner in our household. He picked it up by participating in the community of practice.

The apprentice member of a community exists at the edge of the community taking part in what Lave and Wenger term 'legitimate peripheral participation'. Legitimate because 'in order to be on an inbound trajectory, newcomers must be granted enough legitimacy to be treated as potential members' (Wenger 1998: 101) and peripheral because it 'provides an approximation of full participation that gives exposure to actual practice' (*ibid.*: 100).

The following portraits show people who are, similarly, members of several communities of practice, sometimes fully integrated and sometimes towards the margins. Each community of practice values literacy practices differently. These, in turn, are tied up with a sense of personal identity and the role we play in that community of practice.

If we simply picture learning as something that happens in the classroom, then we can see many adult literacy learners as poor learners. If we see it as bound up in social activity we see something different. Recognising literacy practices as embedded in communities of practice makes an exclusive focus on specific skills inadequate. Teaching skills are important; but we need to ensure those skills are contextualised. Learners should have the opportunity to adopt new or adapt old practices within the communities of practice they inhabit.

Portraits

Sam

Sarah Chu

Trowbridge, the county capital of Wiltshire, is one of a group of small industrial towns surrounded by rural villages and within commuting distance of Bath, Bristol and London. The population (some 30,000) is predominantly white. There is also a large Afro-Caribbean community, a significant Turkish population a smaller Chinese and Thai community and the largest Moroccan population outside London. A number of national companies provide factory work.

Sam was sixty-eight years old and had lived with his wife in Trowbridge since arriving in England from Jamaica in the 1960s. For over thirty years, he had worked as a baker for Bowyers (a large local employer of factory workers). He had six children and fifteen grandchildren, some of whom lived in the Trowbridge area and others in America or the Caribbean. He was a Christian and a very active member of his church. He had begun attending a literacy class I taught at the College in September 2002 after he had become the chairman of the social club in the community centre, on the recommendation of some of the club's members who were among its students.

I asked Sam to be involved in this assignment primarily because I knew that he led a very full life. At this stage, however, I had no idea exactly how busy he was and how many times literacy was embedded into his activities and life. When I discussed it with him, he said that he was privileged to be asked.

Sam evidently saw the literacy class as something to be enjoyed and relished; he had no particular interest in gaining accreditation and qualifications. At the same time, it emerged in our conversation that he did not really view what he did in his daily life as using literacy; to his mind, literacy meant learning, and learning took place in a classroom.

After speaking to him, I felt that his literacy practices could be divided into three areas: religious, socialising and personal relationships. At first I was undecided whether to use the term family or personal relationship literacy. I decided on the latter because 'family literacy' left out of the picture the strong relationships which Sam had with other people outside his family.

The church and his faith were very important to Sam. Almost all his activities outside the home were related to it. Its members were people of mostly Afro-Caribbean descent with literacy practices grounded in the Bible and reading Scripture. Sam used these literacy practices to create his own literacy events. For example, he copied a passage of scripture from the Bible but used his own interpretations to create a speech he gave to church members. The words used were familiar to him and passages that he had heard countless times he could probably have recited by heart.

He told me that he wanted to "exalt" and thoroughly enjoyed leading the praying. Before leading the session, he would use his time to make sure he understood the meanings and feelings expressed in the passages. If he were asked to produce this work independently, it would prove to be a very difficult task for him. Instead, he used what he could say fluently and comfortably to produce a piece of writing that expressed what he wanted. Two examples he gave me illustrate this. Until the previous year, Sam had been the president of his local men's fellowship group at the church. This group met once a week and involved a discussion session or Bible study. He still led the session and prepared speeches that he gave to the group. One evening, the group produced an advertisement to promote their fellowship. This was produced using a computer. Sam did not do the writing; what he did, was discuss what he wanted the advert to say with another member of the group who then used his computer literacy to produce the text. In other words, Sam used his oral confidence to get help for doing the written work. Another text, a rota for the men's ministry was also a joint effort between Sam and a member of his group. For this he wrote what he wanted to appear and his colleague typed it up, correcting any spelling errors on the way.

The second area where literacy was embedded in Sam's life was in socialising outside the family. The church was the centre of his life and his socialising was interlinked with it, but it was a different kind of activity. As I mentioned earlier, Sam was elected chairman of the social club. This met every Thursday in the community centre. He had been instrumental in increasing the number of the group and spent a lot of his time planning activities that would interest them – knitting, dancing, flower arranging and day trips – relying on his confidence and personal friendships to organise these. It was also from this group that the literacy class developed, to which he was keen to recruit others. He set up a luncheon club that met once a month. For this, he would handwrite the menus which (he said) he was happy to do, as they were simple and only for a small group to use.

Once a month the committee met and discussed what he had planned. He would give the ideas and his much younger colleague would produce the written text: an advert, a form or information; another example of Sam and others producing texts in cooperation. I would be hesitant to say that Sam did this to avoid writing. He liked to talk and be with other people and in each event each person had a role: as the speech giver, writer or person who can use a computer. We could describe these as networks and in fact they are, but they are unconscious links and cooperation that had developed over time.

The final area that I have categorised is personal relationship literacy. Sam had a large family, living in the UK, America and the Caribbean and a number of close friends living in Trowbridge. He was seen as someone who helped others; he filled his life with activities and people. He saw his family in the UK on a regular basis and wrote infrequently to his children and other family members abroad. He was writing less and less, he told me, because (he said) it was so cheap to phone and that was what he preferred to do. He and his wife helped each other with any writing and reading that came into their life. The main reading that he did on a daily basis was the Bible and he read passages that were familiar to him. (I don't think he would recognise the words out of context.)

Sam: husband, father, grandfather, uncle, friend, organiser, spokesman, student, motivator, planner, leader and Christian. His social network was rooted in the church and his literacy practices came about through his interaction with the members of the church, his friends, and family and also with me as his teacher. He needed a literacy class to help with his writing. However, when we look at his networks and his life it seems that he was happy and led a fulfilling life. He enjoyed his class as a social occasion; he also practised his writing. As a literacy practitioner, I saw the gaps in Sam's knowledge. As a person who knew him, I saw the full and happy life he led.

Moze

Mandy Weatherett

My case study was not selected; I asked for a volunteer and Moze was the only learner to come forward. Initially, I was a little disappointed as I had hoped to interview a native English speaker and Moze was from Israel. I also knew very little about her as it was only her second lesson. However, she provided a fascinating insight into her life and the difficulties she faces as a bilingual person. She had acquired, rather than learned, her spoken English and had had limited educational support to help transfer this language skill to paper. She therefore had little explicit knowledge of the rules governing grammar and spelling. Her writing reflected the informal style of everyday speech, and lacked the clear sentence patterns associated with standard written English.

Moze was happy to be known by her nickname, though I changed the names of her family and friends. My initial interview was conducted in the neutral territory of a bar and lasted about an hour and a half. I then spoke to her briefly about her social networks before my presentation to the course group, to confirm that the information I was presenting was correct. We met again socially when we clarified some of the issues raised in the presentation and discussed her poems. This time, her boyfriend, Tim, accompanied her. At his suggestion, we looked through the draft of the report together.

Moze was a 30-year-old Israeli who had moved to UK with her English husband in 1998. She had since divorced and lived with Tim in Old Town, Swindon.

Hebrew is the official language in Israel, and English is taught from the age of ten. Moze spent her early years living near a Youth Hostel where she socialised with English and American youths. By the time she reached ten, she spoke English 'street talk' very well and saw no need for the ABCs of school English. She rapidly became bored and was excluded from class for using bad language. From ten to 13, she spent as little time as possible at school, though she enjoyed the challenge of homework and exams. In Hebrew she did well, much to her parents' surprise. Her spoken language was apparently fast and often grammatically incorrect, but her strong sense of competitiveness pushed her to work hard for the tests.

Despite good results, the school could not ignore her absenteeism and she was asked to leave at the age of 13. Apart from a brief time in a school for troublesome teenagers and, some years later, an incomplete course on Fashion Design, this was the sum of Moze's formal education.

She did attempt to return to school at the age of 15, but it was a school for troublesome teenagers and Moze felt she was gaining nothing and left shortly after joining. Some years later, a boyfriend persuaded Moze to attend a course on Fashion Design, but this ended with the relationship. Since then Moze had had little formal education. She said that she disliked being within a 'frame' and classroom settings evidently felt like a barrier to her learning.

Moze continued to improve her English in a social environment, using it as a medium for discussing personal matters. 'Real communication', she felt, required English, and Hebrew was reserved for more formal communication. She was keen to identify with a cultural tradition different to her own and, in doing so, consciously distanced herself from her own cultural identity.

When she first arrived in the UK she began ESOL classes at Swindon College, but her spoken English was superior to that of the other learners and she felt that her individual needs were not being met. The catalyst for her return to the college in 2002 was being turned down for a bilingual post in a company which traded with Israel. She felt that her written skills had let her down. Her primary reason for joining the class was to develop her vocabulary and improve her writing.

Moze's workplace regularly changed as she took temporary positions. She had just finished a three-week stint as a lorry driver and said that the notices on the wall were occasionally a problem. These usually informed employees of social events that would be taking place. Moze was too embarrassed to spend a long time reading notices and always missed the 'get togethers'. The only writing she had to do was filling in where she had been, where she was going, a date and a time. If anything more was required, she said she would 'cheat' and resourcefully look into other situations for the words she needed and, occasionally, write in a way that hid a misspelling.

Since the age of nine, Moze had kept a book of her poems, the earlier ones written in Hebrew and translated to English were accompanied by an illustration. Some of her later English poems had a Hebrew translation on the facing page: an interesting counterpoint to Moze's claim that she could only express herself in English. All the poems had personal themes and related Moze's history and her feelings at the time.

During the process of her divorce a friend had helped her with the paperwork. Whenever possible, Moze enlisted Tim's help with official documentation. She said that she was able to do it, but there were less likely to be mistakes if she handed it over to him. He also helped out if there was anything of importance to read. Again, Moze could have read it herself, but she felt that she was slow and that it was a waste of time when he could do it more easily.

At the same time she made a concerted effort to improve her vocabulary by reading, which was pretty well self-taught. As a youngster she had been taught the basics at school, and then forced herself to read beginning with a comic called *Archers*. She said that the pictures didn't interest her; her aim was to learn how to decode the text. In recent years, she had read a few Danielle Steele books, but found that they were all pretty much the same. She was trying to read John Grisham, but said it was slow. If she found difficult words she tended to skip over them and only returned if she couldn't get an overall picture of what was happening. She did not particularly enjoy reading but persevered with the novels as the language was familiar. She did not attempt to read newspapers as she had problems with multi-syllabic words.

At work, Moze avoided situations which might cause her to linger over reading a text. She did not ask for help but, whenever possible, she used existing texts to aid her spelling. She refused to carry a dictionary as she felt this would be an indication of weakness, and she would never publicly admit to having difficulties. As she said, she 'would rather stop than fail' or appear to fail.

Tim played a dominant role in Moze's circumnavigation of literacy difficulties. Whenever he was available, she would enlist his help in decoding, summarising and writing. When he was not around, Moze could manage if she had sufficient time, and she had devised the strategies already outlined to overcome or disguise more immediate difficulties.

Moze's social network had changed since her divorce. It was now limited to a small number of people, but it was not a dense network as few of her contacts had mutual relationships. Tim was obviously a pivotal figure in much of it: supportive of her learning and willing to adopt the role of literacy mediator, he knew some of her other contacts, but rarely socialised with them.

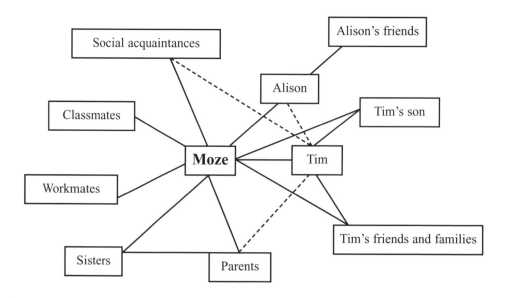

Moze and her network

At weekends, Tim's seven-year-old son often stayed. In this relationship, Moze's status was not clearly defined and she was not involved in the daily literacy practices associated with parenthood. However, despite her feeling that his level of written literacy was often higher than her own, she did occasionally get involved with his homework.

Tim and Moze frequently socialised with his friends and their families. Moze regarded herself as a 'tomboy' and was more comfortable mixing with 'the guys'. However, in situations where the families gathered, she did not participate in conversations as they often discussed places or things she was not familiar with.

Her own family in Israel consisted of parents and two older sisters. She saw her parents once or twice a year and phoned them weekly. Their English was very limited and all communication was in Hebrew. This altered the balance of power when her parents visited the UK, as Tim was only able to communicate through Moze. Moze considered herself the 'black sheep' of the family and had never got on very well with the sisters. Contact with them was infrequent and distant.

The only other person whom Moze regarded as anything other than an acquaintance was Alison. They used to meet regularly for a drink: contact had lessened in recent months because Alison would quite often bring her friends along. On these occasions conversation tended to revolve around hair, nails and children, all of which were of little interest to Moze.

Moze's reluctance to participate in social events such as these with less familiar associates was interesting. Her explanation was that she had no background knowledge, or interest in the subjects discussed. This was undoubtedly the case, and was very probably exacerbated by her differing cultural perspective. She told me English humour was very different from her own and, consequently, difficult to understand. With the additional hurdle of following a second language spoken at natural speed, Moze could well have faced difficulties interpreting deeper meanings and deciding on an appropriate response. Faced with such situations she would withdraw.

Moze's only other relationships were uniplex, and had little impact on her daily life. Her work was temporary, communication with workmates limited and she had little inclination to socialise. In class, she joined in discussions and chats with her classmates, but she did not meet anyone outside the classroom. She had a number of acquaintances that she had met over the previous five years, but meetings were never planned, and conversation was limited to civilities.

Moze had an unusual combination of strengths and weaknesses and these would have been viewed very differently in the two cultural environments she had lived in. In Israel, her command of the English language was considered an asset and her fluency admired by both English and Hebrew speakers. American English was a powerful influence; she had mastered it so well that she was able to convince strangers that she was Hispanic American. She became an intermediary between her native culture and the non-native population and as 'broker' she was very much in control. In England, her social context and subsequent roles had changed dramatically. To some extent, Moze now worked on a deficit model of literacy, as she was often judged, and certainly feared being judged, by her inabilities rather than her abilities. Because of her oral fluency, she was viewed in much the same light as a native speaker with a similar level of literacy competencies.

Standard English is the dominant language of power and Moze found herself reliant on her boyfriend to provide this. The combination of his role as her mediator and her restricted social network was ultimately disempowering for her: a situation that she was highly motivated to change.

Pauline

Karen Bilous

The language of 'problems', 'limitations' and 'serious consequences', ascribed to those without the skills set out by the International Adult Literacy Survey (IALS) (OECD 2000), has very negative connotations. It gives rise to metaphors of 'disease' (Barton 1994: 13) and ladders to be climbed (Crowther, Hamilton and Tett 2001: 2) which are quite outside the contexts in which people actually use literacy.

According to the English Adult Literacy Core Curriculum standards which grew out of the IALS report, Pauline was not functionally literate. Yet she had dealt with literacy events in different domains throughout her life: work, family, community and church. Each domain was different and over time the way in which she dealt with these events had changed. She was now 46-years-old, married, with three children at the time of this research. Her employment record was one of success, having been promoted on a number of occasions. She had participated in community activities and had been an active member of ecclesiastical life in her community for a number of years. Yet, because of her lack of reading and writing skills, she was on the 'bottom rung' of this 'socially constructed deficit model' as she was not:

> functionally literate ... one of the reasons for relatively low productivity in our economy, [something that] cramps the lives of millions of people.'
> (Moser 1999: 8)

It seems that the definition of illiterate and literacy takes on different meanings depending on how the government of the time defines it. It had been only very recently that Pauline had felt her life 'cramped' by poor literacy skills. In her interview with me about this, she told me that she had left school with little confidence, having been told by teachers she was 'stupid' and 'thick'. Yet once in employment, with strategies to overcome her imperfect reading and being a productive member of staff, she no longer felt either stupid or thick.

When she married she did not tell her husband she did not read. If there were any reading or writing required at home, she would leave him to do it and just sign her name wherever necessary.

On this last point, Pauline was adamant. In 22 years of marriage, she said, her husband 'didn't have an inkling'. Pressed, she then told me a story of her recent change. A tax form had arrived with her name on it and she completed it herself before her husband got home from work. She said, 'He became quite huffy with me,' and that later on that night when they were in bed, he had said to her, 'You don't need me any more.' She reassured him that, 'My skills or lack of skills have never been a deciding factor in my needing you.' It is as if there had been an unspoken agreement in the marriage, by which he was made happy when he was able to do things that she was unable to do for herself. Now that she was emerging and taking control of her literacy, the power balance had changed.

During the interview, Pauline reflected on the 'consequences' of not having good literacy skills. Whenever her children asked for help with their homework she would say things like, 'Go and ask your dad, he's better than me at that,' or 'I haven't got the time' and would deliberately start to absorb herself in some housework. When they had been little, her shortage of skills in this had not really bothered her. It was as they were getting older that she had become more self-conscious.

Whilst they were small Pauline had gone back to part-time work as a carer and home-help for the elderly. She also became chairperson of the local playgroup. She told me that she had a reputation for being 'good at delegating', a strategy she employed to avoid situations such as having to read or write minutes. Her reason for not engaging in other village activities (e.g. quiz night at the pub, drama club in the hall) she said was due to a lack, not of skills, but of interest in these events.

After she joined the local Evangelical church Pauline's life (and literacies) changed radically. One day in Bible reading class, the leader asked for a volunteer to read out loud. She asked Pauline to read first but Pauline refused. After the class the leader took Pauline to one side and explained that her son was dyslexic and that she had suspected that Pauline was as well, as she recognised some of the characteristics. She made the initial contact for Pauline to attend a basic skills class. In our interview Pauline said it was not until she had started to attend the Bible reading group that she had really missed being able to read. She was a gifted artist and at first she had gone home from its meetings and translated what she had taken from the readings into pictures, but she became unhappy about not being able to communicate as others were able to, i.e. through the written word.

A term after she had been attending basic skills classes, Pauline saw a job advert in her local shop for a kitchen assistant at the local school. She applied for the job and was successful. Later she took a food hygiene certificate and went onto work as assistant cook. She had to read a range of information in work, such as fire regulations and procedures, recipes, first aid procedures, etc.

Pauline was exceptionally pleased to be able to engage in a number of other literacy events and practices that she would not have attempted in the past, such as reading the rotas for flower arranging, welcoming or tea, the information on the many notice boards in the church, and completing forms for jobs, tax, etc. The event she was most pleased about was that she read Psalm 150 out in church, without having had time to rehearse it. This was the very first time she had attempted anything as public as this. The reaction from her fellow congregants was, she told me, very positive.

The 'addicted readers' amongst us find it hard to imagine going through life without being able to read posters, signposts, personal mail, newspapers, etc.

> We are struck with the feeling of how deprived we would feel ... how lacking our lives would be . . . how disadvantaged we would be ... (Mace 2002: 5)

These days, Pauline told me, 'I can't imagine going around and not being able to read words on everyday signs and things.' It seemed she had now gone full circle and joined the 'addicts'. At the same time, it seems from my interview with her that she had begun to feel a 'lesser person' when in a situation where she compared her lack of reading and writing skills with others. Most of her life had been spent quite happily without these skills but domains change over time. It was only when the importance of the different domains shifted from her early oral domain of work and community involvement to the written word of the Bible that Pauline felt 'cramped' and decided that she wanted to climb the ladder of the core curriculum.

At this point in her life she had a more positive outlook about her abilities and was using the strategies she incorporated over the years to help dyslexic children to overcome their barriers to learning. She felt she was having a positive input into their lives and felt more fulfilled as a person.

Joyce

Gillian Knox

I interviewed and talked with Joyce on three separate occasions. I had expected to find that she had a lot of help with literacy practices from her immediate family and that none of her hobbies or interests would involve reading. Instead I found that she was fiercely independent with regard to her personal affairs and had established a personal network from which she was learning and gaining confidence in her literacy skills. This is how she described her day and her aspirations (recorded by means of Language Experience)[3]:

I get up first thing in the morning and watch GMTV and watch Trisha.[4] And then I go upstairs, get washed and dressed, put on some washing, do some housework. I make some breakfast for my husband about 12 o' clock before he goes to work. Sometimes I go shopping if I need to. I usually leave it to the afternoon. I can do what I like in the afternoon. I see a couple of friends sometimes. Sometimes I make tracksuits. I look after my godson sometimes.

I come to college once a week to improve my reading and writing. I would like to sit down and read a book. I would like to be able to sit down and write a letter when I want to. I would like to be able to spell before I do this. I want to see whether I can do it because I always put myself down because I think I can't do it.

Joyce was 47, of Afro-Caribbean origin (born in this country) and had been assessed as having learning difficulties associated with dyslexia. The area of Swindon where she lived was one of its five most deprived wards, with a predominance of low-rise council housing. In terms of facilities, the area was very poorly provided for and there were no sports or leisure centres in the immediate area. There was a library, a small shopping precinct and several community centres which serve as a focus for the community.

Joyce said she often visited the Community Centre to look at the notice boards "to see what is going on." I visited the centre myself and collected three items which were displayed on the information table: from church, education and community organisations. The publishers of the leaflets clearly assumed that their intended audience could read; and in the case of the Church leaflet, could read and understand a specialised vocabulary (confirmation, ecumenical, lay minister). This is language unique to a domain: just like that used in the New College leaflet (Microsoft, CLAIT, flexible learning, computer driving licence) and the flyer published by 'Human Neighbourhood Project' (community cohesion, advocacy, mentoring, inter-generational partnerships, sustainable human cities).

When I showed Joyce these leaflets that I had collected, she immediately picked up the computing and church leaflets; she was curious to see what information they contained, and began to skim through them of her own accord. I was surprised at her confidence at doing this, since she had always maintained she couldn't read. Yet here she was, scanning through the leaflets and making comments to me about the information they contained. As she was skimming the computer leaflet, she told me that she wanted to learn how to use a computer and

---

[3]   For a full account of language experience, see Mace 2002: 186–197 and Mace 2004.
[4]   Daytime chat shows on ITV 1.

she was seriously thinking of joining a class. Joyce was probably confident to look through these leaflets because they were a part of her domain and of interest to her; she wanted to find out what was in them.

On the other hand, she showed no desire at all to read the 'Human Neighbourhood Project,' probably because the vocabulary on the front of the leaflet was unfamiliar and therefore the subject matter appeared to be outside her sphere of interest. Coming into contact with an unfamiliar domain can have the effect of excluding the reader/writer because he/she is not familiar with its language/ values. In retrospect, I wonder whether she would have been more interested if I had explained the content of the leaflet in plainer language.

Joyce informed me that there was a library in the area which I visited to find out the literacy practices involved in joining the library. As soon as I walked through the doors I was struck by the bank of notices and social sight signs in front of me, many of which were prohibitive or warning notices. I was then taken aback by the information demanded on the library application form. In the past I have used a library form as a "simple form" for students to practise their name and address, but this one proved to be a prime example of 'a complex social practice imbued with issues of identity'. (Fawns and Ivanič 2001: 80). Not only did it ask for name and address, but also for information on ethnic origin and answers to questions such as *"What made you decide to join the library?"* This may be all too much for an individual struggling with literacy and he/she may decide that filling in the form is too much bother. It is also a good example of how literacy domains and the different social practices demanded by different institutions can cause a conflict of interest. On the one hand the library wishes to encourage people to join, but the bureaucracy demanded by government policies may have the opposite effect.

Invited to tell me about her literacy practices, Joyce told me that she kept a list of family birthdays on a piece of paper and the list contained names and dates to help her write the birthday cards. She also said that she copied the names on the card and then added her own, without adding a personalised message. She used her diary to write in hospital appointments, kept phone numbers on a piece of paper at the back of it along with her National Insurance number, but said she didn't keep a written diary because she felt that her poor spelling let her down. She was quite surprised when I pointed out that because she was the only one who would ever read her list, it didn't really matter about the spelling.

She also told me that when money was tight, she would occasionally write a shopping list. She usually shopped without a list, but when she did this she tended to spend more. Interestingly enough, she painstakingly copied the items she needed from the packets and tins in her cupboards. On the rare occasions she went out she would write short notes for her husband.

She didn't write letters because, as she put it, "my spelling lets me down". To keep in contact, she used the phone whenever possible. If she really had to write, she used simple words she could spell. Any letters she received she tried to read for herself, asking her husband for help if she got stuck, but I got the feeling that she would only do this as a last resort. If there was a newspaper in the house she would have a look through it and read any bits of interest. She tended not to use a television guide but flicked through the channels to find out what was on.

In 1991, Joyce was diagnosed as being diabetic. This was before she started basic skills classes and before she was assessed as having SpLD associated with dyslexia. She said that the nurses in the diabetic clinic gave out literature on how to control and cope with the diabetes, but at the time she wouldn't own up to not being able to read and so didn't read it. In retrospect, she wished that she had tried to understand it so that she could have controlled the diabetes. It wasn't until the diabetes got so out of control and she ended up in hospital, that her sister-in-law intervened and tried to help her read and understand information from the British Diabetic Association.

As a consequence of her ill-health, she had to give up work. Her inability to understand the literature in effect cost her her job. When her insulin levels rose again, she resolved to do some more reading on the subject. We agreed to do some work on this in class. She had to learn another kind of specialist vocabulary so that she could be more confident to read around the subject independently.

She also had to complete official forms to do with claiming disability allowance. For help with these, Joyce turned to a disabled friend who had been through the process herself. She viewed this arrangement as a partnership, 'We puzzle it out together' she said, and the friend completed the blank spaces with the agreed response to the question. In return Joyce provided company for her friend, who lived on her own and was often lonely. They went on outings together.

Joyce had also built up networks around her hobby of dressmaking. She had a couple of friends who sewed and who would help her follow the pattern when she got stuck. When we were looking at the sewing instructions together she explained that she now knew what 'the grain line' meant and could read this on the pattern. She had never made up the pattern we were looking at, but had enough confidence to have bought the material. She looked forward to the prospect of wearing the dress.

Joyce's husband helped her read her letters, but from talking to her I sensed that she would much rather have worked out the reading for herself because in this way she maintained her independence and privacy. If her husband was not around she would ask her eldest son who had a house of his own but with whom she was in close contact.

Joyce definitely felt at a disadvantage when having to cope with certain literacy practices. It can be seen from the samples of texts to which she was exposed that she was presumed to have a higher reading ability than she possessed. She was also expected to be able to write fluently and well (library form, disability allowance form, Christmas and birthday cards). If Joyce had access to her networks, and to people she knew and trusted, then she could cope, but she did not like to display her difficulties publicly. Barton, (1994: 11) talks about a 'deficiency' theory of literacy: 'If an individual is thought to have difficulties with reading and writing then he/she is talked about in terms of *handicap, ignorance, incapacity, deprivation.'* Joyce seemed to think of herself in these terms. She felt that she could not own up to the diabetic nurse that she could not read because of a fear of appearing stupid and ignorant. As a consequence, she had suffered deterioration in her health and had been obliged to give up her job.

This study, however, showed Joyce to be anything but *'deficient.'* On a day-to-day basis she was able to manage her life and had developed a series of networks to which she could turn to for practical help – networks in which she included me, as a source of help in dealing with the specialised vocabulary associated with diatetes. These networks had given her confidence and were helping her to 'grow' as an individual. Her next door neighbour, for instance, had told her about a scheme whereby she could use the money from her incapacity benefit to 'rent' a specially adapted car to help her get about. This had set in motion a series of literacy events. Joyce was now investigating this possibility, but it meant she would have to learn to drive. In order to find out what costs would be incurred she stopped a driving instructor in her street and asked him whether he did a discount for disabled learners. He gave her a leaflet with the telephone number of the driving school and Joyce's next step was to ring up to find out more information. Her experience of filling in the disability benefit form had also given her the confidence to advise another neighbour about *his* disability allowance.

My research for this assignment showed a paradox in Joyce's position. Yes, she had built up a network of support to help her in her everyday literacy practices and yes, this support did give her independence and the means to grow and learn as a person. However, the fact remains that our society is one where mainstream literacy practices are a fact of life and we must participate in them in order not to be excluded. We all turn to others for help to fill in that difficult form or make sense of that difficult text, but most of us can cope with the "small" literacy practices (filling in enrolment forms, writing notes, reading timetables). It is when we can't do these "small" things that self esteem and self worth plummet. Joyce missed the *immediacy* of reading and writing which so many of us take for granted. As she said in her initial statement, *'I would like to sit down and write a letter **when I want to**.'* She wanted to be able to cope without having to resort to the help of other people. Being dependent upon other people meant she had no privacy; improved literacy skills would give her autonomy over her own affairs.

Ruth

Clare Griffin

Ruth was a 50-year-old woman from Jamaica, the fifth of twelve children. As a baby, she told me, she had been handed over to an elderly lady to foster as her mother was ill. She missed her family and would often cry 'in the garden' so as not to upset her foster mother. This separation, she felt, hindered her education. After her mother died, her father left to live with another woman and the family was cared for by her 16-year-old sister.

Life was hard. Ruth was obliged to work, feeding the pigs and fowl, fetching water and packing produce for market either before or during school time. Ruth started school at five when others started at seven and she was unable to keep up. She was frequently beaten for being late and, although she really wanted to learn, she left six years later with very little literacy. She then did a variety of jobs, including sewing, domestic and factory work, and looked after her foster mother until she died.

She had three children whom she brought up on her own. Her daughters grew up to have successful jobs; her son was studying. One of her children lived in Grand Cayman, the other two in Britain.

Three years before this study she came to Britain to live with her daughter in order to help look after her grandchildren as her daughter was ill. They lived in a prosperous part of Bristol on a large modern estate.

Literacy practices change. As McNaught argues, they 'vary over the stages of a person's life ... are not constant ... arise at different intervals, in different intensities and forms' (cited in Castleton, 2001: 58). In Ruth's case, this variation was most dramatically seen in the contrast between her childhood in rural Jamaica and her adult life in urban Britain.

I will briefly summarise here what she told me about the former. In her childhood home, there had been very few literacy events, and no books in the house. Along with many other people, her foster mother was unable to read and write and relied on a network of contacts and the Church when literacy impinged on her life. It was customary and acceptable to sign your name with an X. Her foster mother, according to Ruth,' 'did not have it in her that children needed education'. However, in spite of bad experiences at school, Ruth was determined to learn and taught herself to read by reading things around her. Later she went to literacy classes. However, she always tried to hide her lack of literacy and was very shy. People considered her 'boasty' (stuck-up). Her main support network was her family. She worked mainly in factories and domestic work where no literacy was needed. Once she had failed to get a job as an office junior because she was unable to fill in the form.

When she had her own children, she made sure that they succeeded at school. She found out what homework they had, sat down and helped them and was 'aggressive with them'. She went without herself to get them books and extra lessons. She even took on a support role for other local children, encouraging them round and feeding them while they did homework, so that in spite of her own lack of literacy skills she provided them with what they needed for their own.

In her life in Britain at the time of this study, Ruth was surrounded by literacy events and practices. Her family was highly literate and in some respects her role with her children had reversed; they all encouraged and helped *her* with her literacy. Each one seemed to take on particular literacy events. She told me her son-in-law made her read the paper to find out what is going on; her son helped her with her Bible studies, sometimes reading and discussing the Bible with her; and her daughter concentrated on helping with writing.

Ruth, however, wrote her own letters to her family and friends, now spread over the world. As her sisters and brothers knew of her literacy level, she did not worry about spelling and grammar. As far as other household tasks involving literacy were concerned, the rest of the family dealt with these. Ruth sometimes helped with the shopping but preferred to leave it to her daughter and son-in-law as it was hard for her to find what she wanted.

In two other ways her children took an active part in her literacy events. Although she had a Jamaican driving licence, she needed to take the test in Britain; so she read the Highway Code and Driving Test Theory books and her son tested her on her theory. She had been trying to get residence in Britain and had many forms to complete for the Home Office, which her daughter demystified for her and helped her to deal with, insisting, however, that Ruth wrote the form herself.

Education was highly valued in the household. One of her main roles, just as it had been when her son and daughter were themselves at school, was to provide the support for the next generation to develop their literacy. Two daily events were reading to her grandson and helping her granddaughter with her homework. She also took the children to school and attended open evenings.

Important literacy practices in the household were linked to the Church. Ruth read the Bible before breakfast every day and the *Word for Today*. Although the readability level of the Bible is high, she explained that she coped well with it because she was familiar with the names, terms and phraseology. She attended services twice on Sunday and three evenings a week. She also went to Bible class. Here the members read verses of the Bible, studied handouts and took notes on the discussion. They had to produce a written piece for the following week.

Ruth found this rather more difficult and did not feel able to hand anything in. As her church colleagues did not know of her literacy difficulties, her support network was her family. Her daughter helped with the spelling, but Ruth still lacked the confidence to give the work in and read it out. This inability to admit her lack of literacy to the church elders seemed to be clearly linked to the power relations between church and congregation, teacher and pupil. However, amongst her personal network of friends at the church, she was able to offer support and share knowledge as an equal without revealing her literacy needs.

This reticence was echoed in her attitude to the Bible conventions she attended. She was keen to learn and would have liked to evangelise, but lacked the confidence. You 'have to know the Bible good', she said. At the convention she had to read and discuss the Bible in seminars. Her goal was eventually to go to the Bible College in London. For this she would need to be able to write extensive notes and essays.

The third domain was her sewing class at a project in St Paul's, Bristol, called Silai for Skills. She learned pattern cutting which required her to read instructions. The instructions were often complicated and difficult to follow and her fellow class members supported her with the reading. In return, Ruth offered expertise in sewing, using her knowledge to interpret the patterns.

Commentary

What these portraits have illustrated is the strength of people's social networks and how they are generally based on reciprocity. Sam clearly illustrated how an adult literacy student does not see what he does in his everyday life as literacy. For him, literacy was something that happened in the classroom. This is a portrait of a man who was very involved in his local community and church: an organiser and an innovator, who had access through his social networks to people who were good at literacy tasks. Composition was often a communal affair with people taking on the roles that they were good at. So for Sam, accessing these networks was not about compensating for a deficit of skills, but an ordinary way of being.

However, coming to a literacy class changes those networks, which were never static to begin with. In Pauline we had a portrait of a very capable person, who also belies the image of the adult literacy learner with a deficit of skills. Her case study illustrated both how roles within networks can change and how this can result in a shift in power, which can be disruptive to existing relationships. The portrait of Ruth also shows how roles within the family can evolve, as her children supported her in her learning as she did them when they were young. It is a picture of differing attitudes to education over time and cultures. The communities of practice illustrated here, of family, church and sewing group contrast values and attitudes. Ruth's sense of identity can encompass her family knowing about her difficulties with literacy, but her creation of a social identity doesn't allow her to share her difficulties with fellow church members.

Moze's is the story of a bi-lingual learner who was already very competent in oral English skills. This story illustrates how individual language is influenced by the social networks that are the background to the language learning and how the values we attach to different languages relate to our sense of identity. As with other case studies, this shows something of the importance of the literacy broker in confronting official paperwork and how this is tied up with power.

In Joyce we see how people can use their social networks as a source of learning, illustrating Lave and Wenger's theory of learning being involved in social activity. Like Karen Bilous, Gillian Knox uses the concept of domains to talk about the literacy and language aspects of different communities of practice. Lack of access to the literacy practices of the health service had devastating effects on Joyce's battle with diabetes. However, Joyce's story also illustrates the reciprocity in social networks recorded by Fingeret. Having sought help from a literacy broker with official paperwork, Joyce then becomes an advisor to someone else who needs help with forms; Gillian Knox recognises how she, as teacher, has become part of Joyce's network.

Social networks allow learners to contradict the picture of the 'illiterate' adult as someone not participating in society successfully, and provide us with pictures of people integrated into supportive communities of practice to which they contribute.

What these portraits have also illustrated is how context affects literacy practices: for example, Ruth is able to turn to her family and sewing group for support in literacy practices, but is unable to do the same in her church. The next chapter explores more fully how context, which we have termed the literacy environment, shapes individual literacy practices.

Chapter 3

Literacy environments

Ellayne Fowler

An attempt to explore the literacy environment is an attempt to uncover the different literacy domains of a person's life. This exploration can range from a record of the visual literacy environment to a detailed account of literacy events in a specific domain. The literacy events are crucial, because it is in a person's interaction with their literacy environment that we can uncover the broader literacy practices in which they take part. In this chapter we look at different ways of recording or theorising the literacy environments that people inhabit. I look at this through the concepts of literacy domains and of different literacies. I also explore ways of analysing a visual record of the literacy environment and finish with the concept of a third space between competing domains of literacy practice.

As with social networks, there is a range of meta-language used in this area by our writers, so I will begin by defining these terms and looking at how they overlap. By exploring specific literacy domains it is then possible to see how detailed accounts of situated literacy events uncover larger literacy practices and the values and power attached to those practices. (Barton and Hamilton 1998: 7). The case studies in this section illuminate a range of vernacular literacy practices which exist in some very distinct literacy environments.

We need to first define what we mean by literacy environment. This is a broad term we have used to refer to the printed and written text in our lives and our interactions with it. Barton and Hamilton use the term **domain** to talk about the distinct areas of a person's life, such as home and work, where different literacy practices are required. As with social networks, this concept seems to have its roots in sociolinguistics, where Joshua Fishman used the concept to explore the language choice of bilingual speakers.

Janet Holmes includes a useful definition of Fishman's concept: 'A domain involves typical interactions between typical participants in typical settings' (Holmes 2001: 21). Fishman used institutional domains, such as family work, education and religion to explore how and where people used particular languages. According to Fishman:

Consciously or not … members of speech (and writing) communities utilize such major social institutions, and the situations most commonly pertaining to them, as guides for navigating through the unpredictable currents of interpersonal communication in bi-lingual situations (Fishman 1989: 235).

The idea of speech-and-writing communities takes us back to the idea of communities of practice and to the larger picture. In exploring language or literacy domains we are not simply assessing someone's language or literacy skills, but trying to see how they fit into larger social practices.

Mary Hamilton (2000) discusses how investigation of visible literacy events can help us to infer the literacy practices involved. This also gives us an analytical process we can share with learners to raise their awareness of the literacy domains in their life. Hamilton uses similar elements to Fishman (participants, settings, artefacts and activities) to explore pictures that address literacy events. Hamilton defines these as follows (2000:17):

Elements visible within literacy events (*These may be captured In photographs*)	Non-visible constituents of literacy practices (*These may only be inferred from photographs*)
Participants: the people who can be seen to be interacting with the written texts	The hidden participants – other people, or groups of people involved in the social relationships of producing, interpreting, circulating and otherwise regulating written texts
Settings: the immediate physical circumstances in which the interaction takes place	The domain of practice within which the event takes place and takes its sense and social purpose
Artefacts: the material tools and accessories that are involved in the interaction (including the texts)	All the other resources brought to the literacy practice including non-material values, understandings, ways of thinking, feeling, skills and knowledge
Activities: the actions performed by participants in the literacy event	Structured routines and pathways that facilitate or regulate actions; rules of appropriacy and eligibility – who does/doesn't, can/can't engage in particular activities

We can explore this idea more fully through an example. I was considering the idea of the literacy environment as I wrote this at home in a study that is full of texts, either on the walls or on shelves or on surfaces. This is hardly surprising in this particular location in the house. However, when leaving the house via the kitchen door you would pass our fridge which acts as the house notice board. This literacy setting is in a communal part of the house. It is visible and prominent and you have to pass it to enter and exit the house (see figure below).

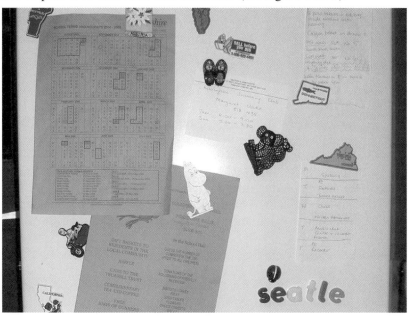

Literacy event	Literacy practice
Participants: none visible in the photograph	*Hidden participants*: Someone wrote the instructions for the washing machine and someone added to them. Someone has made a name with the plastic letters. Who printed and altered the school timetable and who brought it into the house and put it up?
Setting: A kitchen in a family home in a rural area of England	*The domain of practice*: family, but the educational domain has intruded through many of the notices
Artefacts: Photocopied timetable, handwritten instructions, plastic letters, fridge magnets with names on	*Values, understandings, way of thinking, feeling, skills and knowledge.* Why has someone spelled out **seatle** and is there a letter missing because of lack of spelling skill or lack of letters? What do the instructions tell us about who uses the washing machine – who is the expert in the family who has written the instructions?

Literacy event	Literacy practice
Activities: Using magnets to put up notices, taking them down, moving magnetic letters around.	*Structured pathways*: Who is allowed to put things on the fridge and who decides to take them down and why. What can and can't be put on the fridge?

By exploring the questions in the right hand column we can start to uncover the typical routines and social practices of this specific family domain. For example, we could look in more detail at artefacts. My nine year old son spelled out SEATLE (*sic*), because his father was going on a business trip there. He tends to use whatever letters are on the fridge rather than getting more letters from the pot on top of it. He often makes new words with his friend in the morning on the way to the school bus (new, as in made-up or interesting, never from the school spelling list). You could see this as an example of a school practice being subverted into a vernacular practice.

The washing instructions have been on the fridge for years. They are for my husband, who has amended them with important information about separating the wash into dark and light clothes. This is a reflection of the roles within the household, traditionally related to gender. My husband regularly does the washing, but the instructions are still there. He says, 'It is not in my normal mind-set. I always check even now'.

This analysis also highlights some of the difficulties with this type of research. Hamilton, in her work on media images that include literacy, points out that, 'What counts as an 'interaction' between people and texts turns out to be problematic' (Hamilton 2000: 26.) Sometimes the written text can be present, as in my example, but 'no active literacy event is taking place' (*ibid..*). Indeed, if I had included anyone in the picture they would probably not have been interacting with the text on the fridge, and yet those texts do have significance. Hamilton suggests:

> We need a form of description that acknowledges that people can participate in literacy practices in a range of ways, some of which involve a very passive role. By the same token, what seem to be inert texts in the background of an image, can be active in a variety of ways in shaping and signifying the meanings of social practices (ibid . . .: 32)

Indeed, a good example of this follows in Gill Whalley's portrait of Chris and how he interacts in complex ways with safety notices in the workshop.

Another difficulty in analysis can arise from the concept of **domain,** which may be why we've used a slightly looser term of environment. **Domains** frequently cited in literacy and sociolinguistic studies include work, home/family, education and religion. However, these domains are not necessarily as static or located in space as they seem (see, for example, Tusting, Ivanič and Wilson, 2000). Domains can overlap significantly, as in the portrait of Rachel which follows, where work and home are located in the same space on a farm. In this situation, domain becomes defined by the literacy practices (such as official agricultural form filling vs personal letters), rather than the other way round.

Another way of conceptualising this socially situated view of literacy, again from the *New Literacy Studies*, is the idea of multiple literacies, based on Brian Street's concepts of autonomous and ideological models of literacy. An autonomous model of literacy is one that sees literacy as a set of skills that is separate from the learner, which can be codified. The English Adult Literacy Core Curriculum is a good example of a product of this view of literacy. While it goes some way towards acknowledging the importance of the student's context and how this impacts on learning in the introduction and in sample activities, this curriculum remains at base a hierarchy of skills that we impose on literacy learning, independent of learners themselves. (Hence, for example, being able to spell the 'days of the week' appears at a lower level than being able to spell 'months of the year'.) In addition, in order to explain how a person's knowledge and ability in reading and writing may vary, the teacher is asked to use the concept of learners having something called a 'spiky profile' of skills. Yet, as Street points out, 'if literacy is a social practice, then it varies with social context and is not the same, uniform thing in each case' (Street 2001:18). In contrast, he poses an 'ideological model of literacy':

> ... literacy not only varies with social context and with cultural norms and discourses regarding, for instance, identity, gender and belief, but ... its uses and meanings are always embedded in relations of power (Street 2001: 18).

This is sometimes conceptualised as **literacies**, which vary with context. We can, for example, talk about 'essay text literacy' to talk about the sort of literacy that is valued in Western society. This is a literacy that is based on academic writing, against which all other writing is often judged and found wanting. If we conceive of literacy in this way, our investigation of domain could become clearer. We are looking for typical literacy practices used in that domain, but it doesn't preclude us from recognising when literacy practices move out of their usual setting. When homework is done at the kitchen table, for example, academic literacy enters the home domain.

It might be more useful to talk about literacy practices rather than literacies, but either term enables us to explore the concept of **vernacular literacies**, that is those literacy practices that are often undervalued as they don't conform to essay text literacy. However, they involve typical ways of doing and making meaning that a newcomer to the particular community of practice would find confusing. Anyone who has walked into a betting shop for the first time, for example, would struggle to fill in the betting slip in a way that would be accepted practice, for example. In that situation, a 'literate' person could find themselves struggling with that particular literacy (Barton and Hamilton 1998:141). In this case, someone else who is familiar with this domain, but who also happens to be an adult literacy learner could be 'more literate' than their teacher: an expert rather than the sum of deficits he or she is figured as by an autonomous model of literacy.

For all the difficulties stated, the exploration of someone's literacy environment or literacy domains can produce rich results for both learner and teacher as the following studies illustrate.

In their research in Lancaster, Barton and Hamilton explored in detail the vernacular literacies of the home domain. They divided these into six categories:

- Organising life

- Personal communication

- Private leisure

- Documenting life

- Sense making

- Social participation

Many of these practices were evidenced by the literacy texts in the home. For example, in terms of organising life:

> Much day-to-day practical organisation involves literacy. People have notice-boards for details of appointments and social activities; also calendars and appointment diaries, address books and lists of phone numbers. Within the home there are places where letters, pens and scrap paper are kept. Different sorts of books are kept in different rooms and the order on the shelf may be important, reflecting particular classification systems. (ibid..: 248)

You can explore this in your own home domain. Do you have a notice board? What is on it and who puts it there? Does anyone update it? What does that tell us about roles in your family? Notice boards are often a public space, even within the home, that can tell us a lot about the values, roles and relationships of the people using that public space. Who gets to display on or control that space can also tell us about the power relationships involved.

A number of research studies have looked at contrasting literacy practices between home and school. Shirley Brice Heath researched three local communities in the South-eastern area of the United States. These were a mixed middle-class community (she called Maintown), a white working-class community (Roadville) and a black working-class community (Trackton). Heath's work showed how children from the latter two communities came into school without the mainstream literacy practices developed in Maintown and were therefore educationally disadvantaged, as the Maintown literacy practices were the ones used in school. Part of the research included clear documentation of the literacy environment in the different communities:

> In Roadville, babies are brought home from the hospital to rooms decorated with colourful, mechanical, musical, and literacy-based stimuli. The walls are decorated with pictures based on nursery rhymes, and from an early age, children are held and prompted to "see" the wall. Adults recite nursery rhymes as they twirl the mobile made of nursery rhyme characters …In each Roadville home, preschoolers first have cloth books, featuring a single object on each page. They later acquire books which produce sounds, smells, and different textures or opportunities for practicing small motor skills … Reading and reading-related activities occur most frequently before naps or at bedtime in the evening. (Heath 1994: 81)

This shows how it isn't enough to simply record the environment, but also it is necessary to record the interaction. From this detail at the micro level Heath was able to infer the larger literacy practices and to demonstrate the mismatch with school practices. Once we are aware of that mismatch changes can be made to allow all children equal access to the educational system, although often the changes are in the child. Hence, for example, an emphasis on a pre-school education that is formalised in a curriculum and which prepares a child for school. There are fewer examples of the school changing to suit the child.

Another way of investigating the visual nature of literacy in the environment is Anita Wilson's ethnographic work in prisons. She uses the concept of a *third space* to talk about how people, including the researcher, make a space for themselves within the institution of prison. This *third space* is positioned between the practices of the prison and the outside world. Wilson uses a picture of a pillow, covered in writing to illustrate how a prisoner can construct a third space: 'This pillow itself is taken out of its institutional role and re-located as a site for graffiti, conventionally linked to outside world activity' (Wilson 2003: 298). The vernacular literacy of graffiti is re-sited within the institutional domain of prison. This raises issues of power, as Wilson notes:

> In one statement, 'John Lomax' has chosen to place himself as a person – and name both himself and the object of his affection – even though this act will identify him as damaging the property of the institution, an offence which carries with it a substantial punishment. (ibid.)

Wilson also notes how texts can take on meaning beyond the messages contained within them when they are used to decorate and personalise prisoners' cells:

> In addition to posters, photographs and correspondence, prisoners use books, certificates, magazine articles and personal items to make up a visual

image of how they wish to be seen. (ibid..: 305)

Often these materials link more to the outside world than prison. Here exploration of the literacy environment shows how these literacy items relate to a sense of identity.

Exploration of the literacy environment can take a number of forms. We can explore literacy domains, identifying typical literacy events and inferring literacy practices from these. We can establish different literacies, such as *essay text*, *betting shop* or *cooking*, which are linked to distinct domains of life, but may occur in a range of localities. Through analysis of the visible literacy environment we can detail literacy events, again allowing us to establish the more global literacy practices involved. Those practices also uncover the power relationships and sense of identity tied up in literacy practices. Within the context of adult literacy the exploration with a learner of their literacy practices in different domains of their life should help to develop truly SMART (specific, measurable, achievable, realistic, time bound) targets based on an accurate picture of not only what a learner can already do in terms of skills, but how those skills are used and embedded in social practices.

The following profiles offer portraits of contrasting literacy domains encompassing both home and work. Often there is a blurring between the line of home and work with studies based in the army, on a farm and in a convent. We also visit a veterinary practice, a college and a Wiltshire town.

Portraits

Chris

Gill Whalley

Chris was an 18-year-old construction student who worked as a carpenter in a local firm and attended a Further Education college one day a week to follow a construction course. He had fallen behind with his coursework and as a consequence I had been working with him for one hour a week on a one to one basis, offering learning support within the college. He was often dismissive both of the value of reading and writing and of his own abilities: *'I can't read but I only need to, to do these books and then I never need bother again'*. He was actually far more skilled than he ever gave himself credit for. In the context of the college, however, he approached course work, reading and writing tasks with anxiety and negativity.

Chris's attitude to reading and writing interested me. In this case study I set out to examine the reading and writing he did in his everyday life, the value it represented in those different contexts, and who he looked to for support if he encountered problems. Starting from the premise that reading and writing are not just skills but socially situated practices, I wanted to explore several themes: what, with whom and when, Chris actually wrote and read in his everyday life, the networks in which such literacy events took place and the particular roles he took in those contexts. The theme of 'networks of support', that is of literacy as a resource which is shared in a community became significant.

I discussed the assignment with Chris before one of his individual support sessions. After he agreed to help me, we then met for 30 minutes before his next session and continued this pattern for the next three to four weeks. Initially, I used the framework for the assignment as a basic interview schedule, but working over several weeks, I was able to pick up on information we had not covered or to pursue topics further. Equally, Chris was able to reflect and think more about questions in the interviewing period and he sometimes initiated discussion, as he became more engaged and interested in what we were talking about. He seemed to enjoy talking about his wider everyday life and while I worried about the ethical dilemmas, and dangers of asking potentially intrusive questions in an unequal relationship, I attempted to address this both through trying to provide feedback and by placing our discussion topics in a wider, more general context. For Chris, helping me with my work, as I helped him with his, was positive.

Chris lived in a close-knit community. He had lived on the same estate all of his life, had gone to the local comprehensive and worked around the corner from the local college. His uncle ran the shop on the corner of the road and he socialised with the lads he went to school with. He lived at home with his parents and two younger brothers who were also keen football players. Most evenings he enjoyed going to a local social club: '*A lot of my mates go there. I get on with everybody there. It's friendly. Everybody knows everybody*'. At the club he played snooker and was organising a football team.

Chris had a full life and juggled work and college commitments. He was able to keep times and dates in his head and didn't feel the need to write them down on paper; although he sometimes scribbled key times he needed to remember on the back of his hand. While he would send birthday cards to people in his family, he regularly saw all the people important in his life so he didn't need to write to maintain communication. Initially he struggled to think of times when he would write outside college. Formal letters that needed answering, e.g. from the bank, he preferred to respond to verbally and he would always visit rather than write a reply. Most of the letters, adverts and general organising in his home, e.g. correspondence regarding his brothers' football matches, Chris said, '*Mum would see to*.' Such tasks were almost seen as 'part of housework' while letters/forms to do with his car, Chris would ask his father to help him with. While Chris was very negative about his writing, '*I just can't write neat and I can't spell*', he was very aware of the power of his signature in negotiating with the outside world: '*You just need to know where to sign your name.*' Much of the information Chris needed to operate within his environment he could get through his dense network; he didn't need to read. He was 'told' about his job and about the college course and in making decisions about clubs to visit or football matches to attend he relied on verbal feedback. His primary source of information would be his friends and not the written word.

What became very quickly apparent in Chris's discussion of reading and writing acts was how sociable these were. Many of the reading and writing acts he described took place either with somebody else's support or on a communal, shared basis. He enjoyed reading the magazine *FHM* for instance and would often do so at a friend's house where they would read together. He also enjoyed reading the sports pages of *The Sun* and did so at the sports club in the evening where men of all ages dropped in and would read the sports pages together. While in a different work context, reading was a source of tension for Chris, in this one, it was a source of pleasure and fun; any difficulties eased over: *'They might have a laugh and take the mick but someone will help. We'll read it together and have a laugh'.*

Chris was in the early stages of setting up a football team at the club and had identified a friend to help him who would deal with all the reading and writing this might generate. He was pragmatic about this: writing and recording might be necessary to do things 'properly' and he had already identified someone who was 'good at that sort of thing.'

Within Chris's immediate social world he was active, skilled and engaged in a range of interests. Within college and his work environment he was far less comfortable, however and in these contexts reading and writing was seen as threatening. This was how he described how he coped: *'I keep myself to myself, just keep my head down.'* At work, as a carpenter, he had developed a range of strategies to avoid exposing what he perceived to be his 'weaknesses.' One of his tasks was to read the insurance briefs on jobs. To avoid having to do so publicly or have to do so 'out loud' in front of others, he always claimed he had read it earlier and therefore already knew the brief. He would then informally 'chat' to his colleagues about the task and through his comments and jokes ensure that he had all the information he needed. This complex, highly skilled behaviour meant he didn't have to confront a reading task in a social context in which he felt vulnerable.

In a similar vein, reading *The Sun*, particularly the sports pages, was a lunchtime ritual at work. As I have said, this was something he enjoyed doing at his club. Here at work, it evidently felt very different to him. The same sports pages that he looked over with his friends no longer felt so easy: *'I just go and sit in my car by myself at lunch time. I don't want to struggle and them to see that I can't.'*

In a relaxed setting Chris could effectively read and understand *The Sun* but his perception of the act was shaped by the social context. Work carried the risk of public scrutiny and 'failure'. Such literacy acts then became threatening and imbued with power. His strategies of withdrawing to avoid potential embarrassment were effective, however, Chris was choosing when and with whom he wanted to read.

Chris saw his job as a carpenter as one *'where I don't need to bother about reading.'* In reality he operated in a visual environment where notices, instructions and posters were all around him. A quick tour around the college workshop he attended one day per week illustrated this and we discussed the resulting photographs. Chris was familiar with all of them and was able to explain what you needed to read, what you could ignore, when particular notices might be significant and where they might be situated. Much of the reading in this social context was through inference and a complex reading and interpretation of the clues given by particular words and images. Tuned in as he was to this environment, his attitude to such literacy was again pragmatic: such reading events were purposeful, meaningful and functional. Meaning was achieved partly through informal discussion with others, and through informally learning the rules of the social environment in which this literacy was embedded: *'You pick it up from doing the job ... You know what you need to read and what you can ignore.'* In this context literacy is an intrinsic, 'taken for granted,' part of the visual environment.

For Chris college coursework represented schoolroom literacy with formal demands, imbued with power, and threatening failure. Literacy events, however, were embedded in his everyday life and were meaningful, enjoyable and pragmatic; enabling him to do what he needed or wanted to do. Such events were often in interaction with other people; interactions which were usually enabling and supportive.

Chris's social network was important to him and offered him a variety of literacy support: with reading letters at home and the more formal literacy demands of running a football club. Verbal communication was his most important source of information. It was perhaps only if this network were to be disrupted or as he speculated, if his role were to change, that his literacy needs might change: *'Perhaps if I wanted to start my own business then there might be things I needed to do that I needed help with.'*

Chris actively chose to withdraw from such literacy practices which threatened or might label him in ways he was uncomfortable with. In the context of the workshop however he was a skilled and sophisticated reader of the written material that surrounded him. In his everyday life literacy was a part of the social world he shared with friends and a means by which, with support from others, he got things done. Exploring beyond the official discourses around literacy into the social realities of people's lives enables us to recognise not only flourishing literacy practices but to acknowledge the creativity and complex communication skills that people already possess.

Vicky

Karen Bell

When I first interviewed Vicky I was very taken with her commitment and determination. She had failed to turn up for our first appointment. When I saw her the following week she explained why. She had only just moved to the area and her home was approximately forty minutes away from the college. Unable to read the road signs, she had got very lost. In spite of this, the following week with a friend's help, she had tried again.

During the interview Vicky explained how improving her literacy would help in all areas of her life, but that what she really wanted to be able to do was 'sit in a park on a sunny day, with a can of lager and read the paper.' I found it interesting that her main drive for improvement was not work, but leisure. She also said that she enjoyed travel and wanted to be able to map-read. This is how she chose to describe herself in the pen-sketch she wrote for me:

> *My name is Vicky Brooks, and I have just moved to the area to Lower Slaughter. I used to live in Leicester but got offered a new job in horse care. I am working as a groom at the minute but training to be a nurse.*

> *When I am not at work I enjoy my two dogs, socialising with my friends, swimming, horse riding and going dancing.*

> *I am keen to improve my reading and writing so that I can visit my friends in the car because I can't map read or read signs, to go travelling, and to read a newspaper.*

Vicky was 22 when I met her and had recently started working as a groom in an equine veterinary clinic. Although she could read common and frequent words she struggled to decode unfamiliar and longer ones (such as those in road signs). I wondered how she managed with the drug and treatment names at the clinic.

During my first discussion with her, she concentrated mainly on the literacy events and practices surrounding her work. It was harder to draw out of her any literacy she encountered in her home domain. This seemed to reflect Barton and Hamilton's point (2000:12) that vernacular literacies are less visible than more official ones. For Vicky, her work literacy seemed more dominant and influential in her mind.

Although she had been diagnosed dyslexic, I found it interesting that she still apparently felt a need to hide the fact she struggled with reading and writing. Many Basic Skills students that I have met have found the 'label' dyslexic a huge relief and it has enabled them to 'come clean' about their difficulties. While talking to Vicky it became clear to me that she worked on a 'need to know' basis, for example, when registering at a new doctor's surgery. As she wanted to see the doctor immediately there was a form she had to fill in there and then, so she asked the receptionist to do this for her. If there had been a choice, she would have taken the form home and enlisted a friend's help.

Vicky lived in a little village at the equine clinic where she worked. Although the village is attractive and picturesque there is very little to do. There are no shops, just a hotel and a water mill. To shop or socialise she would go to nearby towns. In her spare time she enjoyed walking her dogs and horse riding, at work and with friends.

Being a groom at a veterinary equine clinic meant that Vicky worked in an environment with regular and structured literacy practices that had to be recognised and acted upon. There were set rules for procedures and documentation; every horse that was treated at the clinic had a form accompanying it. This stated all the owner's and horse's details. Information from this was then transferred to the hospital record sheet. This sheet was also used to record all drugs and treatment carried out. Vicky had managed to avoid filling in either of these forms. She used strategies such as being too busy or having wet hands to get someone else to deal with them. If a horse was being given a common drug, such as Bute, Vicky recognised the word by comparing it to that on a label she recognised. She always asked the vet to complete treatment records for her and checked verbally that she had understood the medication and treatment required.

Vicky told me she would love to have been able to read the record sheets so that she could tell the owners how their horse was progressing and feel more confident in her job. There was also a daily diary that she was supposed to read to see what needed preparing on what day. As Vicky was unable to read the diary, she always had two stables ready at all times, just in case.

Vicky had a range of social relations; she seemed to have a person to help in most areas of her life. Once she had been diagnosed dyslexic at school her mother went to college to learn more about dyslexia and how to support dyslexic learners. Her father and brother were also dyslexic. Any private letters or text that Vicky was unable to read she would take home to her mother. The friend she shared a house with helped with the day-to-day post and literacy she struggled with.

At work, her boss was aware that she had difficulties. Apart from him, only one friend at work knew, and he helped with the paperwork as much as possible.

When I brought up Arlene Fingeret's idea of reciprocity and mutual exchange (cited in Mace, 2002: 35), Vicky seemed perplexed as to what she offered those who acted as scribes and readers for her. I felt terrible, imagining that I had made her feel inadequate in her friendships. However, after some thought, she said she made them laugh and was always there for them.

For Vicky the literacy practices in her work domain were the treating and caring for horses. The texts involved were required to be completed and read in order for the horse to be cared for correctly. The written text was the starting point but it was integrated into a range of non-text based systems. She used images such as pictures and logos on medication packets and feed sacks. Although involved in this literacy practice she had managed, to a certain extent, to use strategies to avoid these specific literacy events. The discussions Vicky had surrounding the text allowed her to be part of the events and practices.

The fact that her work practices were shaped by literacy events, e.g. forms, diaries, instructions, without which the clinic would not function, reflected the social practice theory of literacy. Her personal response shows me how such events may extend beyond the written to include the spoken word and visual imagery.

Rachel

Jackie Winchcombe

Meet Rachel: a petite woman, with dark short hair and brown eyes, who was what my mother would call 'well turned out'. When you talked to her it became clear that she was articulate, sensible and practical with a good sense of humour. She lived and worked on a farm in Wiltshire and had been coming to adult literacy classes for just over a year.

I asked Rachel to participate in this research because I was mystified about several things. Firstly, I was interested to know why she had decided to join a course known as "Improve your reading and writing". She was 58 years old and had evidently managed until then without feeling the need to come to college. Secondly, she was evidently very committed, attending nearly every session and working very hard at home. Thirdly, and most interestingly, she was a very keen writer, particularly of stories and events that had happened to her. I wondered what was driving this writing, why she wanted to record these events and what intentions she had for the pieces of writing in the future.

During my research I had three interviews with Rachel. The first gave me a personal picture of her, her family life and something of her educational history. We discussed why she had joined the course at this point and I explained to her that I needed her to think about all the things she did in which reading and/or writing played a part. We talked about this at the second interview and she was surprised at the length of the list we made together. The third interview took place after the course mini-seminar and thanks to some good ideas for questions from my colleagues I felt that I got closer to the reasons behind her writing and to what she would like to achieve in the future.

Corsham is a small town of some 12,000 inhabitants situated on the main A4, about 20 minutes from the city of Bath. Officially a Cotswolds town, its honeyed stone buildings have more in common with the elegance of Bath and its cobbled street of weavers' cottages, together with its pretty gift shops, make it popular with tourists. Essentially rural, it benefits from being within a stone's throw of the M4 and a mainline railway station with regular trains to London. It is an affluent area and property prices are high, due to its proximity to Bath where the housing prices are second only to London.

At the centre of Corsham, at a staggered crossroads is the post office and card shop/sweet shop that seems to be a focal point for community life. It is an attractive building, (unlike most post offices), with a distinct 'olde worlde' charm and is always very busy – a queue of at least five people is usually waiting outside at 8.55 am. The post office offers a large number of services, advertised in the side window display, most of which require some reading or writing, if only a signature. Rachel collected her parents' pensions from here on a Friday lunchtime after class. When I asked at the post office what this would entail I was shown a small tear-off slip that she would need to sign. The post office also advertises local services such as the Honeypot playgroup. Interested parties might need to be able to read these adverts, although the images give a good idea what they are about and being able to record the phone number would allow you to find out the rest.

The Town Council offices are directly opposite the post office. Outside the offices is a glass-fronted noticeboard which details the planning applications coming up on the council agenda. If you don't want to venture inside the imposing entrance, reading this is one way of finding out when your neighbour's planning application, which you might wish to object to, is being discussed.

Walking down the High Street you pass The Royal Oak pub which has a board outside advertising the jazz nights for which it is well-known and further on there is the Tourist Information office with a huge window full of posters for local events such as 'Lunch on the Lawn' at Corsham Court – truly 'the big house.'

In the small shopping centre there is a three-sided noticeboard built around a large tree. On the benches surrounding it, people tend to congregate to chat. The board intrigued me; it appeared that anyone can use it to advertise services, events or information, without charge and without having to ask permission. Official notices from the District Council are side by side with every other sort of notice you can imagine.

Rachel lived outside the town on a farm. It was a beautiful location but isolated; she had nobody nearby to chat to over the garden fence. She had three adult children; one girl who had left home to run a branch of a well-known building society in Dorset and two boys who lived at home and helped on the farm. Rachel was a farmer's daughter and a farmer's wife. She had lived in this area all her life, had always worked on the farm and had never taken a job outside. When I asked about the degree of reading and writing needed to run a farm these days she said that it had increased enormously in the last 20 years and was still increasing. For example, the Foot and Mouth epidemic had made it necessary to complete several forms for animals to travel with 'passports'. However, she also said that she did not really get involved with the farming paperwork as this was done by her husband and sons.

Together we made a list of the things she did regularly which required reading and writing:

Phone messages – These were many and varied as home life and work life were closely connected on a farm due to the location of the business within the farmhouse. Examples ranged from 'phone calls from the vet' or 'the SEB' (Southern Electricity Board) to phone calls from 'the egg man.' Rachel managed to record these by using her own personal shorthand for what she could get down in the time and by relying on a good memory to do the rest. These messages were not left for other family members to read but acted as a memory aid for her.

Greetings cards – Like many women Rachel wrote nearly all the greetings cards sent by the household. She did this by keeping the old cards to refer to so that she got people's names right. She then used the words in the greeting printed on the card in her own message.

Calendar – Rachel kept a calendar in the kitchen which all the family used for recording appointments or important dates.

Shopping lists – Rachel wrote and used a shopping list by using a pre-prepared list from Sainsbury's. She recognised the items she wanted on the list and could copy them down without worry as to whether they were spelt correctly. If she wanted to buy an item which was not on the list she would either use some form of shorthand for it, perhaps its first letter, or she would rely on her memory

Household bills – These seemed to be regarded as the job of the men of the family, largely because of the connections between the house and farm. The menfolk handled the lion's share of the part of the farm that made money and hence the literacy events that went with it. Rachel did pay her own bills, such as a credit card bill, sometimes referring to her daughter for help.

Cooking – Rachel enjoyed cooking and did use recipes to try out new meals. Like her knitting she could usually decode the recipe because of her prior knowledge of the subject which helped her to make an educated guess.

All the writing in this list seemed to be embedded in the social practice of what Barton and Padmore call 'writing to maintain the household' (Barton and Padmore 1994: 62).

We also discussed the reading and writing involved in her hobbies, knitting and sewing. Rachel's sewing required little reading because she used pre-printed tapestry which showed her where the colours went. She said that, as far as knitting was concerned, she would be able to decode most of a knitting pattern because of her prior knowledge of the subject. Sometimes, however, with a more complicated pattern this was not possible and she would refer to her mother to get a second opinion. It occurred to me that in this type of social practice, where a skill was involved, reading and writing had less relative importance because other knowledge was also required. It also occurred to me that in this literacy practice I was less 'literate' than her because although I could read the words on the knitting pattern, they had little or no meaning for me.

I was intrigued as to why this capable woman had decided to come back to college to improve her reading and writing. She surprised me by telling me that actually, she hadn't, at least not at first. She had originally come to learn computing. She said to me, 'You know, you sit at home and you think you can fill in the form, but I couldn't.' It was the teacher of the computing class witnessing the 'couldn't' and mentioning to Rachel that the college offered classes in reading and writing that started her off. When I then asked why she had decided to go to computing classes she looked at me in surprise and said, 'To get out, of course!' I was reminded of a time earlier in the conversation when we had talked about social activities and I had asked her whether she went out, say, to pubs or restaurants. 'Oh no,' she said, 'he don't agree with that.' It seemed that learning was an acceptable way to spend one's free time, whereas visits to pubs and restaurants were not, for whatever reason. Rachel joining the literacy group, albeit sparked by the need to fill in a form, was at least partially about wanting some social interaction outside the family and farm.

I asked her if she ever wrote letters, either personal or business. The business side was handled by the men in the family, although it appeared if the men wanted advice that they asked her daughter's opinion. Rachel did say that she would love to be able to write letters to friends and family 'and tell them what I did.' I asked her about the stories that she wrote both at home and in class. She said that these were the sort of thing that she would like to have been able to put into letters.

Rachel's stories were remarkable for several reasons. It might be natural to assume that if a person can't write their address they might not be able to write anything much else. She still had occasional difficulties with her address but ever since she joined the literacy group she had been producing long pieces of writing about things that had happened to her. She achieved this writing by transcribing the words she knew and for the ones she didn't, she just put the first letter and a line. She seemed to want to compose, although the transcribing skills were not yet there to support the composing process. She was not very interested in the fine detail of checking spelling and punctuation but was much more stimulated by working at text level and getting the information down on paper. She always had one piece of free writing on the go all the time and it was the pleasure in writing this which gave her the determination to keep on hammering away at the detailed work.

The people in Rachel's networks, who helped her with reading and writing, were exclusively the family and, to a lesser extent, the college. She could not think of one friend that she would or had asked to help her with a reading or writing task. Some friends knew that she had difficulty with certain literacy tasks but she always went to her family for help or brought the writing into college, choosing certain people to help with different tasks. While her daughter gave advice about any reading or writing concerning money, for example, her mother helped with any reading required by knitting patterns. In this way Rachel was making the most of each person's expertise. What she did for them in return, such as visiting her mother regularly or collecting her pension, was not formalised or recognised as a reciprocal arrangement, because it took place where such things can be an expectation of family life. For example, she provided companionship for her mother by visiting her regularly and doing practical tasks such as collecting the pensions.

To conclude I must, oddly enough, go back to the beginning. I began this case study curious about Rachel because of the contrast between her ability to compose and her inability, as yet, to transcribe very much of her composition without help. For example, she would have difficulty spelling common one syllable words with long vowel phonemes such as 'boat' and 'show' but could structure a story to maximum effect for her audience. I had also seen her begin to use her imagination to continue stories started by other members of the group.

I had been puzzled about the source and reason for her storytelling. I came to see that she saw her stories, like her diary, as the precursor to letter writing and to realise that they might have filled a communication gap brought on by long hours working on her own as a farmer's wife in a wonderful but isolated location.

However, I discovered that Rachel had ambitions for these stories which didn't stop at letter-writing. She was about to be published in the ABE (Adult Basic Education) newsletter and I would not be at all surprised to see her submitting work to local magazines in the future.

Michael

Sue Thain

The British Army has recruited soldiers from the Caribbean and South Atlantic Islands in recent years. As a teacher of Basic Skills for the Army, I wanted to consider how the needs and ethos of the Army as an institution might inform and affect the teaching of literacy skills to these particular soldiers. In this study I examined the literacy practices of the Army and the central role of power within those practices. I also considered the current literacies and cultural norms of a learner and saw how they were affected in this environment.

I had been working with Michael for four months and he seemed keen to be a part of this project. In looking at Army practices I drew on my own experiences; discussions with other basic skills tutors within the Army; interviews with other soldiers and officers involved with the Basic Skills programme and information taken from MOD websites.

I met Michael on his second visit to the Education Centre after he had been sent by his Troop commander. He was a black Jamaican and one of ten children. He left school at the age of ten to work in the building trade to help support the family. He came to England when he was 18, staying with an older brother. After two years in England he was still unemployed. He returned to Jamaica. His lack of a job and a white girlfriend caused a family argument and eventually led to him joining the Army.

He was only barely able to read and write: he could sign his name and pick out numbers and his name from a page of writing. He would not consider reading for pleasure; to him it was a learning tool. He did not have a television nor was he interested in films. However, he loved music of all types, especially heavy rock and reggae. He was not really interested in team sports, but did 'sort of' follow football – because everyone else did. He enjoyed kick-boxing and weight lifting.

Michael spoke Jamaican English. What makes this more complex than many other creoles is the range of variation within the dialect and its relation to the class structure of Jamaica. Linguists use the term 'Post-Creole Continuum' to describe the range of varieties within a Creole. Following creolization a process known as decreolization can occur, where education and social prestige leads some speakers to use a variety nearer to the external Standard. At the other end of the continuum is a local variety with many Creole features (Yule 1996: 234–5). He, for example, would say 'him go school' instead of 'he went to school' and pronounced 'on' and 'and' in the same way. Michael's English was nearer to Creole than the Standard. Within his own culture he had been able to make himself understood and find work. He had not really missed the ability to read and write, because he had a good head for figures and was considered to be very bright and an asset to the building trade.

Michael struggled with tasks where he had to infer meaning. For example, having spent some time talking about a picture of a sign explaining the parking regulations of a car park, I asked him if he was able to park his car there on

Sunday. He replied that he didn't know. I asked him to look again at the picture. He was surprised by the idea that the answer might be there[1].

Michael now lived in Tidworth, in a two-bedroomed house supplied by the Army. (He had an entitlement to housing according to his rank and number of children). The house was part of a large estate owned by the Defence Housing Executive and was part of a deliberate housing policy where all soldiers from a particular ethnic background were housed in the same location. Tidworth is a garrison town on the edge of Salisbury Plain. The Army dominates the town. As well as three large barrack areas, there is a small shopping complex, a garage, a number of pubs, a bowling alley and a leisure complex that is jointly run by the army and the local council. The nearest large shopping towns are at Swindon and Salisbury. Local buses run to both these towns.

All the documentation around daily living, pay statements, medical forms, housing issues were generated by the Army who dealt with them for him. Indeed should Michael have got into debt the Army would take over his pay until it was sorted out. (The Army would see their role as paternal and supportive. It could also be argued that this disempowers soldiers from becoming self-reliant.)

An education officer told me 'Education is an important part of the Army ethos. Soldiers will regularly be *sent* on courses' [my italics]. These courses relate to rank rather than educational requirements; it would not matter whether a soldier was a graduate or illiterate he would still attend the course.

Another soldier extolling the virtues of army system suggested three reasons why he believed it to be an excellent system:

> *First of all, for most of the time the Army is not actually doing its job (i.e. war) so it has time to spend preparing for it. Secondly, it has something of a captive audience. Soldiers sign up for three years and the penalties for leaving are high. That means that the Army has every incentive to train people well – they're not about to leave. Thirdly it is written down. How to do a patrol, how to bed down for the night, what to do when you get fired at. It's all there in black and white. That means that everyone is teaching more or less the same thing every time.*

Army instructors are taught EDIP – Explain Demonstrate Imitate and Practice. Throughout runs the assumption that knowledge is something concrete, codified and outside the learner. Paulo Freire (1994) calls this a 'digestive concept of knowledge' and it assumes that soldiers are empty vessels simply to be filled with useful knowledge.

The idea of 'blocks of knowledge' features in the literacy practices and events of the Army. There is a manual, *Defence Writing*, which lays down how every

---

[1]   This is the author's interpretation. An alternative is discussed in Chapter 5.

document should be laid out and written. A soldier, at relevant points in his career, is taught to speak; give a brief, instruct or give orders, and write in an appropriate manner. Almost every aspect of his or her life is governed by the written word. It would then seem to follow that soldiers would need a high level of literacy.

Michael was obliged to read Daily Orders. These tell every soldier what they are expected to do on that day. Michael adopted a method used by other soldiers who struggle with their reading skills. He was able to pick out his name and the times and dates. Sometimes he could guess what they related to; other times he used this information to check exact details with a colleague or a superior.

Private soldiers are not expected to write very much, except to sign their names. As they move up the rank they will be given instruction on how to fill in all the relevant paperwork. Soldiers are expected to write in block capitals, which from the point of view of developing writing skills may be unhelpful. The need for strict codes informs every aspect of military life and this is also true of its literacies. Michael clearly saw literacy as power and it is this which motivated him as a learner. On this matter his view and the view of the Army differed very little.

Irene

Kate Tomlinson

This is Irene, in her own words:

> *My name is Irene. I am a contemplative nun, which means I belong to an enclosed order. I've lived in this particular convent for 25 years.*
>
> *I'm one of ten in the community and our life is a life of prayer for the world.*
>
> *Our main source of income is distributing Altar breads which are used to celebrate the Mass in a Catholic Church.*
>
> *I enjoy reading and gardening. For an hour each evening we come together for recreation in which we play music, games, art, knitting and sewing.*
>
> *Since I've been made Superior it means I have much more administration work to do throughout the week. This is the reason I am anxious to improve my English and spelling.*
>
> *June 3 2003*

Irene is a nun in an enclosed order of Franciscans, the Poor Clares. This study explored her literacy life in the convent, which exists within the secular communities of Woodchester and Stroud and a wider network of Catholic institutions. From talking to Irene, I knew that literacy practices were controlled to some extent by the rules of the Order. I was interested in the effects of this; I also wanted to learn about the other literacies she used in her life.

My own experience of an enclosed order of Catholic nuns at a boarding school in the late 1950s had made me acutely aware of the specialist vocabulary used by my teachers (mostly nuns) that seeped through the walls from the enclosed 'other side.' We only had glimpses of this in chapel and through spoken references. In Evelyn Waugh's *Brideshead Revisited*, Sebastian explains to Charles that the Roman Catholic Church is not just a place where you go; it defines you as a person. It creates a different world with its own texts and language that inscribe particular attitudes and values. As George Yule (1996) put it:

> *There is a religious register in which we expect to find expressions not found elsewhere, as in: "Ye shall be blessed by Him in times of tribulation ..." It is obvious that one of the key features of a register is the use of special jargon, which can be defined as technical vocabulary associated with a special activity or group. (Yule 1996: 245)*

I first met Irene at an initial interview for adult basic education classes at college. Subsequently we had further discussions about the reading and writing she used in her everyday life. I expected to find a number of changes to the way literacy was used in the convent today but also a context which retained reference mainly to old Latinate texts and its own specialist vocabularies. I made a list of 'prompt' questions for her to reflect on in the interviews. My chief constraints were the pressures on her time, and that I needed a special dispensation to access a community that by definition is closed to all but the nuns. I learned more about the convent and the religious order to which it belongs by looking at a website created by one of the nuns, Sister R. Finally, on June 9, 2003, Irene showed me round the convent which helped me picture where and when literacy events occurred in her life and the rich literacy environment in which she lived.

Irene was 49 and lived an 'enclosed' life which meant that her main activities were contemplation and prayer, separated as far as possible from secular society except for a concern for its spiritual welfare. She was brought up in Cardiff and had had a childhood with domestic problems and a disrupted education. Her parents had died when she was young. Outside her religious commitments, her interests were centred round her remaining family and some friends.

When I first met her, Irene was the Infirmarian at the Convent, looking after the sick and elderly nuns. For this she needed to liaise with the hospital and medical services in Stroud, a town with a total population of approximately 30,000 people. She also had a cupboard in the infirmary stuffed with medicines, and medical instructions she had written referring to different nuns. She described herself as 'not an intellectual' like some of the other nuns, but obviously had a high standing at the convent and wanted to extend her writing skills so that she would be more comfortable with increased demands on them. She was able to cope adequately with most of her current reading and writing.

Shortly after Irene joined an ABE class, the Abbess at the convent died, and rather to Irene's surprise – given her perceptions of her own lack of formal education – she was chosen to replace her. This new role confirmed to Irene that she needed confidence in the extended literacy events that her new appointment entailed. It also showed the value placed by her fellow sisters on qualities and abilities that did not involve literacy, or only the literacy specifically associated with the Church's 'cultural tradition' or 'particular ideology'.

The Convent was situated in a village on the side of a valley south of the semi-rural town of Stroud in Gloucestershire. The 1991 census showed the village to be an exclusively white, solidly middle-class community. Some new housing since that date meant that this had probably increased by a few hundred. For medical, financial and other essential services, the nuns looked to Stroud. This formed part of Irene's 'literacy environment', as did the wider Catholic community of the parish and also the national network of Poor Clare convents. However, the convent itself was the main environment in which she operated.

There were ten nuns between the ages of 40 and 90, each with very specific roles within the community, which acted very much as a family, relying on and supporting each other. Literacy mainly, but not entirely, revolved around religious practices. Reading was for a variety of purposes: private meditation using the Breviary or spiritual texts from the convent library; reading aloud at Mass or to the community in the refectory during meals which are held in silence; or for study purposes. Choice of the latter was at the discretion of the Abbess (from whom Irene had had to gain permission to attend basic skills classes with us) and study activity might include using the computer, doing correspondence courses or attending college. The study had to be seen to serve the purposes of the Order.

The Telegraph newspaper (selected by the last Abbess) and a Catholic national newspaper, *The Universe*, were available for the nuns to read – but only in order to identify objects for prayer (such as the war in Iraq or earthquakes in Algeria or Turkey).

Texts used in chapel had changed over the last 20 years. The Breviary, which is the main one, contains the daily services, including prayers, hymns and lessons. There are three versions, to cover the religious calendar. They are no longer written in Latin, but do contain the kind of Latinate, specialist vocabulary Yule referred to. Certain prayers, often sung, are printed in Latin with a translation underneath. The Breviary used by Irene was translated in 1974. I asked whether she still read the text or if she knew it by heart. She told me that during general prayer she was so familiar with it that she sometimes 'drifted off'. She practised passages she had to read aloud in chapel, in her room. She sometimes focused on a particular word which led her into meditation.

She told me that she had found it quite easy to adapt to the language used, but that this was not the case for everyone and she helped some of the new nuns with it.

'Everyone has trouble reading the Biblical names', she said. She would often offer to read aloud in the place of others who felt uncomfortable doing this, sometimes in exchange for other tasks, such as cooking. Wilkinson (2003) describes an interesting aspect of the way the Church controls and directs the use of reading:

> (Nuns) are encouraged to read the Bible (and other religious writings) in a devotional, contemplative way to bring them into close communion with God. This activity known as "Lectio Divina" (holy reading) does not involve analysing the text. The reader should simply absorb the words and allow God's message to filter through. (p.45)

This was similar to the process used for electing the Abbess, and the role played by words in meditation. The election, by secret ballot as described in the rule of St Clare, did not depend on any job description, but a process of Divine inspiration where, during prayer, names of the nuns which 'came to her' were the basis of further meditation.

Every staircase and doorway in the convent had notes pinned up from people requesting prayers to be said for them. Beyond the main religious thrust of Irene's life, she had several roles that created their own literacy 'domains'. I considered these using David Barton's and Sarah Padmore's three categories of: maintaining the household, communicating with others and personal (Barton and Padmore 1994: 209). As Abbess, 'maintaining the household', she had the role of 'mother' both spiritually and in the sense that she was ultimately responsible for the smooth running of the community. She checked the work of others, such as the Bursar and Sacristan and undertook secular roles such as keeping a guesthouse log book, cooking, mostly using recipe books and helping the elderly nuns with their Christmas letter writing. Interestingly, she told me that she helped them with the 'thinking' – getting ideas for the letters – while they did the actual scribing themselves.

In the second category of Irene's literacy roles, 'communicating with others', there was business correspondence. The convent made and distributed altar bread to other Catholic churches in the area. Irene kept an order book. When she needed to, she would ask other sisters to check the spelling of place names.

As convent Abbess she shared responsibility with the priest for the local parish for receiving and exchanging letters with parishioners who came for advice and guidance. Irene commented that, while others tried to persuade her to learn to use a computer, the priest had pointed out to her the value of 'voice' coming through her hand-written letters. As Abbess, she also linked the convent to the other ten in the country, representing them at the annual Assembly of Abbesses. Before she went she would read and take notes from relevant religious texts and from discussions from which she would eventually help to compile a presentation to be taken round the country. She preferred to remain independent, taking the writing to her 'cell' and working on it slowly with the help of a dictionary, sometimes later asking other sisters to check her English. The Assembly itself provided an interesting example of a literacy network. Irene anticipated the experience with anxiety because of the literacy demands she felt would test her existing abilities. She returned from it full of confidence. Not only had she coped with the note taking, but the President of the Assembly had chosen her and one other nun to write a presentation they would take round to other convents, working as a team.

For Irene, the third of Barton and Padmore's literacy categories, 'personal', included both secular and religious uses of literacy. She wrote letters to her family and friends. She told me that she wrote, rather than telephoned, because the convent only allowed use of the phone for emergencies, in order to keep costs down.

Irene was an example of someone who operated in a variety of literacy domains, some demanding reading of Latinate, specialist texts, others writing letters and notes, both personal ones for herself and for a range of purposes for others. These included messages, numerous reminders to other nuns, formal correspondence with priests, business letters and other bureaucratic form filling and records.

She conveyed to me the sense that she had a well-functioning literacy network when she needed it and was surprised and delighted by the literacy support she experienced further afield at the Assembly. She also, clearly, gave literacy support; reading aloud for other sisters and helping the elderly nuns compose their letters home. She seemed to feel comfortable with many of the literacy events in which she participated on a daily basis, and often preferred to be independent and work things out for herself. The silent, inward-looking image of the enclosed convent community was only one part of the picture I glimpsed. From this brief study I saw the written word being used to reach outwards to a wider world.

Commentary

Chris's story illustrates the importance of context in considering literacy practices. Chris felt comfortable taking part in a reading event, involving the sports pages of the newspaper, in one context but not in another. In each literacy environment (work, home, college and a social club) his interaction with literacy was different, moulded by the different values associated with literacy. Reading and writing here was not simply a matter of skills, but a set of practices moulded by values and power and often governed by the environment in which it was practised.

Vicky's portrait reflected issues of identity and her need to create one other than of someone who had difficulty with reading.

Jackie Winchcombe presents us with a picture of the visual literacy in a town centre. Her portrait of Rachel also showed how the domains of home and work overlap; in this case, on a farm. In her exploration of the literacies of knitting and sewing she also highlighted how the teacher can become the apprentice.

The very specialised literacy practices of the Army also create an overlap between home and work. In the study of Michael, we glimpse a man working to master both Standard English and discourses that are specific to the army context.

Kate Tomlinson introduces us to the literacy environment of the convent, an environment that most of us will never enter. Irene also demonstrated the strength of a reciprocal literacy network that valued the skills she had to offer, to the extent that during the period of the case study she was voted Abbess. Kate and Irene worked together on the research. The next chapter looks at the different ways that this approach to the research process worked for others.

Chapter 4

Research as process

Jane Mace

In the last three chapters, we have been considering the meanings of a social practice view of literacy in terms of: events, practices and values; social networks; and literacy environments. This chapter returns us to the work of researching these aspects of literacy. We look at the methodology and its origins in ethnographic approaches; consider a few thoughts on the aspiration that such research could be empowering in its effects; and lastly note some of the learning to be gained, if not immediately by the research subjects, at least by the researchers.

The spirit of ethnography

Discovering what people want to learn and why is a research process. Finding out what learners already know about a topic is another. These are both what may be called the exploratory stages of inquiry. To this extent, any teacher of adult literacy already engages in research. (Mace 1992: 64–81). In addition, however, in the context of national strategies with targets of improvement to be reached, she or he is called on to spend a lot of time on research of another kind. Initial assessment, diagnostic assessment, reviews of progress and tests of achievement, are all tools of exploration to guide the teaching – but they also contribute to the larger research projects of institution and government: statistical surveys of product (student learning) for funding purposes. Each of these activities involves the teacher-researcher in testing something (the learner's level of ability) against a common set of criteria. All take place in the environment of classroom or office. The person being tested provides data in the form of the answers they give or the writing or reading they do; the teacher-researcher records, codes and files.

Ethnography is research of a different order. Originating as an approach taken by anthropologists, it entails gathering data from a range of sources, including observation and relatively informal conversations; it operates without pre-structured or pre-fixed categories for interpretation; its focus is a relatively small scale group, setting, or even individual; and its analysis involves interpretations, descriptions and explanations, with numbers and charts playing a minor role, at most. Possibly its most striking feature for our purposes is that the research data comes from 'real world' contexts, rather than those 'produced under experimental conditions by the researcher'. (Hammersley 1994: 1–2) In a comment on her own ethnographic study of families and literacy, Denny Taylor suggests that the central thrust of ethnographic endeavour is 'the search for structures of signification in the behavior of others (Taylor 1998: 101). Citing Geertz's contention that anthropological writings are 'fictions' – that is, something made or fashioned – she contends that ethnography, seen in this light, is 'neither theory not method' but rather 'a certain kind of intellectual effort … a venture in "thick description." ' As to her own work, aspiring as it does to 'capture on paper a fleeting reflection of one aspect of informants' lives', Taylor suggests that it:

> might kindly be referred to as field research undertaken **in the spirit of ethnography**. (ibid.: 102) [my emphasis]

This seems a good phrase to use for the inquiries undertaken by the teacher-researchers in this book. The 'reality' of their research contexts was certainly only partial (interviews often took place in the surroundings of classroom or office rather than the learner-participant's chosen or familiar environment) and given the constraints of time, the recording of 'literacy environments' discussed in the previous chapter, could only reveal glimpses. But in that they carried a 'commitment to describing and explaining the social world' (Hammersley *op. cit.*: 14), the spirit of the studies as a whole was unmistakeably ethnographic.

At the same time, such studies fall rather neatly in line with the requirements for adult literacy teachers' professional qualification that we discussed in the Introduction – requiring the ability to evaluate the social factors which inhibit or promote the effective development of literacy. In Appendix 1, we set out the assignment brief that we designed to meet this requirement and some activities we used to develop teachers' research skills to fulfil it. The task enabled them both to explore 'social factors' with learners themselves and gain a practical introduction to ethnographic research. In the context of a policy environment stressing skills and targets, this felt a useful counterpoint to the shadow of deficit models (the frame of reference which says the most important piece of information about the individual man or woman learner is their *inability* to do certain things or their *lack* of skills in particular areas). In theory, at least, for this assignment, the learners were being positioned as experts and guides.

Research and empowerment

At first sight, however, the arrangement seems to have a built-in inequality which would work against any power gains for the learners. Structurally, the teachers are in the more powerful position: as experts, as assessors – paid to know more than those they are teaching. How could the learners achieve any sense of power through participating in their research project? This is a question that faces any practitioner-researcher in adult literacy education. In their report on a national study of learners' views of their progress and achievement with a team of such practitioner-researchers, Jane Ward and Judith Edwards report a concern with the 'power differentials inherent in this research area' calculated to give edge to the researcher in the equation:

> They can, for example, control the direction of the interview, the language used, interpretation of the data and the uses of the research findings. (Ward and Edwards 2002: 56)

This differential was also true for the researchers in this book: with one difference. The teachers who engaged with learners to undertake these studies were themselves in a learning position, not only as researchers, but also as trainees on a course on which they themselves would be assessed. As trainer-educators, we had to work out how to empower them and, in turn, enable them to share power with their subjects.

In saying that members of the first group 'engage with' the second, the preposition is important. The training for this work aimed to show teachers how they could convey a proper respect to the person 'researched'; how they could clarify that the interview(s) were intended to get the interviewee to teach them something of their own life, not in order to assess their skills, but rather to glimpse something of their social uses of reading and writing. The protagonist in the project should not be the teacher-researcher, but the participant-learner. From the way the idea is first described through to the choices made in editing the writing produced out of the work, somehow or other they should be, if not in charge, at least in a guiding role.

In our view, if empowerment is to have any meaning, the research process of these case studies should be of value to the subject, as well as to the researcher who initiates it. Since in this case the researchers are adult literacy teachers, we might imagine that this is just what would happen; these are people, after all, who are used to providing encouragement and promoting self-confidence. But there is a difference between a general feel-good effect that someone might feel as a result of being sympathetically interviewed and a sharpened sense of power as a result of new insight into their life and context they stand to gain if they are involved in the examination of their data.

In this respect, we can find a useful distinction made between research which is 'empowering' and other kinds by a group of academics concerned with this same issue of the benefits to the research subjects:

> We have characterised 'ethical research' as research on and 'advocacy research' as research on and for. We understand 'empowering research' as research on, for and with. (Cameron et al 1992: 22)

Each of these, it is argued, differ from the concern of the positivist researcher with 'observations procured in a scientific manner' capable of generating data with the status of 'value-free facts': working on studies concerned with quantitative results (*ibid.*: 6). Since positivism, as they put it, continues to be the dominant 'common sense' of modern science (*ibid.*: 6), it is worth our spending a few minutes on it here. The approach originates in natural or hard sciences; in terms of social science, it offers precisely a feeling of being more 'scientific' than other approaches:

> Positivism (*writes Martyn Denscombe*) is an approach to social research which seeks to apply the natural science model of research to investigations of the social world. It is based on the assumption that there are patterns and regularities, causes and consequences in the social world, just as there are in the natural world. These patterns and regularities in the social world are seen as having their own existence – they are real. For positivists, the aim of social research is to discover the patterns and regularities of the social world by using the kind of scientific methods used to such good effect in the natural sciences. (Denscombe 1998: 239–40)

A positivist approach to social research expects the researcher to be neutral (and preferably invisible), and requires data collected to be pure of the distortions or impurities of bias. The patterns they see must be out there, objects separate from the observer, facts to be collected and described.

The problem with this, as Deborah Cameron and colleagues point out, is that it leaves out of the picture what the subject observed thinks they are doing. They give the example of a woman digging in the garden. We can see her and describe her, without judgement. What she is doing is clear: it is a fact. She is digging. As they suggest, however, something else could be going on. She could be burying the budgie. She could be letting off steam after a row with her children. She could be relaxing after a hard day at the office. Or she could be worshipping the Goddess Earth by cultivating her. In other words, the *meaning* of what is observed can only be properly understood if the agent's own understanding of what is going on is included (*ibid.*: 11). Social reality, such as what people do with reading and writing, can only be understood to a limited extent by 'objective' observations of human behaviour. For a fuller understanding, values, beliefs and feeling have to be considered as well: those of the observed, and also those of the observer (who might have her own opinions on how well the digging is being done and whether the woman ought to be doing something else instead at the time).

In terms of research into basic skills and literacy, the following example might help us appreciate the issues raised for us if we stay with a positivist approach to literacy use in practice. An example of positivism at work could be the use of a single timed test with a specified choice of answers, to determine the progress that someone had made in their literacy. This test provides information on the person's performance in test conditions, which can then be compared with the same person's performance in the same kind of conditions at a point in time some months before. Adding up many such comparisons and analysing them by means of a scoring system provides numerical results for the purpose of assessing the organisation which provides them with learning opportunities.

These results are needed for this purpose. The problem with the research tools being used is that they ignore the person's performance in any other context than that of a timed test. The approach which is better suited to help with this is the one we have described in this book. It might not be impossible to adapt it for the purpose of arriving at the numerical results needed for organisational assessment. Suppose for example, that in order to explore *progress*, we take the concept of 'literacy confidence' as the topic for learners to provide their own assessment of how far they have come. Apply four grades to it, first at point (A), to score interviewees' answers to a question about 'how, if at all, would you like to increase your literacy confidence?' At point (B), three months later, the same grades are used to code interviewees' answers to the question: 'how much, if at all, do you feel your literacy confidence has increased?' At both points interviewees explore literacy confidence in four or five domains (or roles): work, citizenship, family, recreation.

Here is one possible answer, for one of these roles, at each of the two points, provided by an entirely fictitious person called Rose:

(A)*'In the role of citizen, I really want to improve my literacy confidence in how I deal with the Inland Revenue forms I have got to complete. I feel panicked by the pages and pages of it and keep putting it off.'*

(B) (*Three months later*) *'No, I didn't improve my confidence, I suppose, but I did get the forms done. I got my sister to help me deal with it. We plodded through them together. That's how we do things and it's done now. So I feel great!'*

In positivist terms, the statistic produced by this would be one of *no progress*. No skills had been improved. In terms of a qualitative understanding, however, and one which recognises the literacy as a matter of social relationships, the statistic would be *progress* – because the person concerned felt better about the problem. As far as organisational performance was concerned, the statistics that might result from an approach like this could be interestingly different from those generated by the more positivist research tools of timed tests.

Empowering research, in the terms set out by Cameron et al, treats people as participants in the inquiry, not its objects. What is more, their approach is a deliberately interactive one which may need to attend to the participant's own agenda. In contrast to the positivist approach the interviewer would be expected to clarify that 'asking questions and introducing topics is not the sole prerogative of the researcher' (*ibid*: 24). Arguably, the teacher-researcher should also not only share purposes and reflect on findings with their participant, but also include them in deciding how they interpret them.

Finding the person

This is all very well, but in a short, small-scale project like this, it may be easier said than done. There are pressures. The teacher-researcher only has a few weeks in which to carry out the study, and a first issue facing them is: how to find the person to research with? Should it be someone they already know well, as a learner in one of their own classes? If so, who? This is how Tricia Jones (Chapter 2) answered this:

> *I began this case study by requesting a volunteer from my Friday morning Brush up your English class. I chose Sarah as she was the newest member of the group and, as such, I knew the least about her as a person. When she joined the group a few months before, I had been struck by her determination and tenacity to improve herself.*

Sarah Lyster, in 'Dave' (Chapter 1), also found someone whom she had only begun to know; attracted, this time, by his willingness to speak up:

> *I first met Dave when I started my teaching practice. He was the most communicative member of the group with varied interests and an opinion about almost anything. I decided to ask him to be my case study character as I was intrigued by his literacy needs.*

For Mig Holder, 'pragmatism was the prime driver in selecting the student I would invite to share in this project with me'. She chose Martin (this chapter) as being:

> *someone who I thought would be available and willing to take part. I had no other specific criteria in relation to the level at which the student was learning, or anything particular that I knew about his background.*

Once found, the learner-participants have their own reactions to being the subject of research. Chris Topham, for instance, found that John (Chapter 1) was a little disturbed by it:

> *I explained the project to him and told him it would involve my asking him questions and recording his answers. I assured him that he would not be named and that he had the right to tell me to mind my own business if he chose to. John said he was quite willing to cooperate, but I think he found the idea of being the subject of research a little odd.*

In their case, the project entailed several conversations, including phone calls; as Chris reports, this meant some discomfort for both of them:

> *I tried to ration my questions at each meeting over several weeks and was very apologetic when I felt under so much pressure that I had to ring him at home. During this conversation, he went to the lengths of moving to another*

room so that his wife would not overhear what he said. This made me feel very uncomfortable.

Kauser McCallum and Marie Anne (Chapter 1), on the other hand, met

on two occasions, for an hour or so each time. At our first meeting I shared with her the guidelines for the assignment. She confirmed that she was happy to be involved and chose the pseudonym I have used for her.

The concern not to be 'intrusive' featured as a major issue for teacher-researchers invited to reflect on what they had learned from the project. As Sheila Nicholson put it:

I found problems with my questions being misinterpreted. It was best to ask open questions to get the student talking.

This itself offers learning to the teacher. How can an interview for research be felt to be different from an interview for assessment (or, for that matter, an interview for a job)? Gillian Knox told us that:

Initially I was very unhappy about the assignment. I didn't like the thought of "prying" into someone's personal life to ask them about their literacy practices and networks. I thought this was a terribly intrusive exercise. Nevertheless, despite my misgivings, I gritted my teeth and went ahead.

As things turned out, her subject joined in as an active contributor:

I need not have worried. [She] was only too happy to talk about her literacy practices, her views, opinions and everyday life ... It was very much a collaborative effort and I know from her reaction that she feels proud of the finished product.

What seems to have helped this sense of ease was the deliberate effort Gillian made to share with her subject the research question and areas of interest ('we went through the criteria together section by section', she wrote). As we shall see in the next chapter, the process had gains for Joyce, as well as for Gillian.

Reading and writing

Another part of the research process is that of reading: in a larger project, the 'literature review'. For this project, participants were expected to show evidence that they had consulted some relevant texts and related their own projects to this reading. For people who do not have reason to write academically most of the time, this can be tough. In the original essays, authors summarised and para-phrased what they had read; commented on it and sometimes analysed it; in short, they were critical readers. (As we said in the introduction, the editorial process for this book has removed most of that referencing work, because we felt it would have been repetitive for you to keep finding the same sources cited.)

We also asked the teacher-researchers to write their case studies as miniature research reports: ensuring that they included something about the background to it, their methodology for tackling it, what they 'found' and how they reflected on these findings.

Both these aspects of the work are set out in more detail in Appendix 1. As part of the process of working on these, however, we would stress the value of people doing these studies sharing the work with each other. In course time, we encouraged them to give 'work in progress' presentations and gain feedback from their peers, in the form of encouragement, and extra questions they may not have thought of. This is a really useful stage for any researcher to get to (often taking the form of a 'workshop' in a conference). What can make it extra useful is if each teacher-researcher, when it is their turn to present their stuff, has a colleague in the group willing to scribe for them; stressing that what the scribe is there to do is write down not so much what the presenter says, as the questions and feedback she is offered by her peers. In the anxiety as to how well we spoke, such questions can escape us when we look back on the discussion later; yet these can often be the ones to extend our ideas or remind us of something obvious we needed to include. As Jackie Winchombe mentioned (Chapter 3) such discussion helped her form new questions to enable her to explore things further with her subject.

Listening and looking

The interviews themselves work best if the interviewer has had some practice at doing them – either from previous research experience, or from activities on the course. (Again, Appendix 1 describes one such activity). The one thing that seems important to manage in any research interview is the balance between listening and recording. The key thing we felt needed to be kept in mind is the association for an interviewee of being interviewed by someone who keeps stopping to take notes; an association, all too often, with being in trouble. Mig Holder reflects on this in her work with Martin in the previous chapter. Yet (as her extracts show) verbatim spoken words can often be more expressive of the person than the reported speech captured from notes after the interview is over. One solution can be provided, as it was for Mig, by an interviewee's own interruptions to what he was saying. Another can be for the interviewer to share the problem with the interviewee, and ask them if they could pause to allow them to scribe something of what has been said so far. It's another opportunity to let them in on the process: share the task with them; tell them of the issue, as you see it; and let them check your version of what they have said. A third strategy – as suggested in this assignment – is to ask an interviewee if they would be willing to write about themselves in their own words (with whatever scribal support they find useful). This notion of the 'pensketch' is one which Mary Hamilton and David Barton used in their study of reading and writing activities in Lancaster (Barton and Hamilton 1998: 66). As the examples in some of our case studies indicate, this can offer one more source of insight, for both participants.

Looking at the environment, as we have already said, is the other task which the teacher-researchers are asked to undertake, with the help of their learner-participant. Things get seen with new eyes. The researcher gets the chance to use their *imagination* as well as their observation, in considering what might be involved for their subject in these surroundings, with these texts, and these circumstances.

The pieces we have chosen for this section show the researcher as much in the foreground as the subject, each using different ways of showing the analysis and interpretation of research findings.

Portraits

Jed

Sheila Nicholson

Jed lived and worked in Devizes, a market town in Wiltshire. Born in South Africa, he had moved to England with his parents when he was 13 years old. At some point he had been classified as having special needs. He had enjoyed school, which he attended until the age of seventeen, after which he had taken a three-year catering course at Trowbridge College. There he had achieved qualifications in silver service, bakery and waiting. Despite these, he told me he felt he had learned a lot more since leaving college (having worked in jobs that have involved cleaning, gardening, glass collecting, waiting and being responsible for stock). He enjoyed his present job as a trainee chef because all the staff are young and work well together. 'Work', he said, 'is always teaching me.' The job as a whole involved a whole new literacy practice for him, and he said that he had managed it well.

Not long before we talked, Jed had been given the opportunity to do silver service for four days. Although the waiting staff were not supposed to look over the customer's shoulder at the menu, he had had to do this discreetly in order to write down their order. Each week, he would write down his work rotas in his diary; labelled food products, and noted down the date and time when he had cleaned something. He told me that he would like to work his way up as a waiter in a higher star hotel, and to have a working knowledge of foreign languages in order to converse with customers from other countries.

In his spare time, Jed practised TaeKwon-do, went sailing, and enjoyed cooking. Of TaeKwon-do, he wrote:

> *It is a sort of martial art. I am a red belt going for my black tag in August. It is great fun. We do sparring, patterns, fitness, defence and loads more.*

The black belt involved taking both a practical and a written test, in which each candidate had to say why they want to be a black belt, and what it would do for them.

The sailing he did was with a voluntary organisation providing young men with the opportunity to live and work on board a large yacht. In the course of doing this, he had learned to record the wind force and position of the boat in the ship's log. From his local library he borrowed and read books and magazines on sailing and martial arts. At his computing class, Jed used the internet to find out information on martial arts, and word processed his notes on these. He also sent lots of emails and text messages.

Jed had come to the basic skills class because he wanted to improve his literacy, and he enjoyed attending. He told me:

> *I'm not sure how far I can go, but I want to go as far as I can. I was bad, right down here. I had to pull myself up. I don't know how I did it, but I did it somehow.*

(He pointed to a place fairly near the ground when he said this.) My understanding of these words was that, at a given point in time, he had realised that his life could be a lot better than it was, and he was determined to improve it. He wanted to shake off the label of 'special needs', which he had always lived with. He wanted to be himself, no labels attached.

Jed told me that he felt that he could tackle most pieces of literacy, but if he had something like a letter of condolence to write, then he would ask his parents to help. I asked him if his parents helped him with filling out forms. He said no. The following week, Jed brought to the class an E111 form (entitlement to medical treatment in Europe) which he had taken to the post office three times, each time to be sent away to change something. He had just one item left to correct, and we sorted out what it should be. The point is, he had told me that he did not ask his parents for help with form-filling and yet he had asked for more practice at form-filling. Initially I had felt that these facts did not add up. Now I realised: he did not ask his parents for help, he tried to fill the forms in on his own: that was why he wanted more practice. In this instance, the college had become part of his network, a place where he could fill in forms as part of his work during the lesson, with the support of a tutor. Jed conveyed to me a strong need to be independent and to shake off the special needs mantle that had always surrounded him.

It seems that the interpretation of limited literacy as embarrassing is a concept conceived of by those who are privileged to be 'literate', and who assume that everyone needs to attain the same standards of literacy in order to function fully in society. I was certainly not aware that Jed was embarrassed at attending a basic skills class. On the contrary, I had the impression that he was proud of assuming responsibility for his own learning.

As Crowther, Hamilton and Tett (2001: 2) comment, the usual way to think about literacy is in terms of a ladder that people have to climb up with the emphasis on what people cannot do, rather than what they can. Those at the bottom of the literacy ladder are seen as lacking necessary skills. If emphasis shifts to how adults can, and want, to use literacy, then the focus moves to what people have, rather than what they lack; what motivates them rather than their perceived need. It follows, they argue, that literacy work should be part of a broad education that enables adults to take greater control over their lives and recognises that the fact that they may have imperfect reading and writing capabilities does not mean they are 'incapable of critical inquiry' (ibid..: 109). Jed was striving to take control of his life, and was motivated to attend college because he saw literacy as being a key to this. From this study, I could see that he had assumed a lot of responsibility for his own learning, becoming involved in literacy practices at work and at college, which also served as an important network for him.

What I also discovered was that it is not easy gathering information from someone, especially when (as in this case) I had no background knowledge of that person to draw on. Sometimes I was puzzled by Jed's answers. I subsequently realised that the answers I received depended on the questions I asked, and that both questions and answers are open to misunderstanding. Jed put his own interpretation onto my questions, and I put my own interpretation onto his answers. Fortunately, he was willing to be interviewed on more than one occasion, so that I was able to clarify issues with him. By doing this case study, I was able to relate practical knowledge to the background reading I had done. The study of a learner has brought this to life.

John

Susan Buchanan

I first met John when I was working as an IT trainer. At that time he was homeless and was relatively new to Salisbury. The IT lessons became a big part of his life; he rarely missed one. John's literacy skills were relatively poor and his speech less than lucid and I next came across him when he did a basic skills initial assessment at the Probation Service. It was after this that I asked him if I could use him as my case study; he readily agreed. My intention was to look at his social practices and discover what literacy he used in everyday life. I interviewed him on several occasions, asking him about all the regular events in his life and looking at the literacy therein. I always checked with him what I had written down to ensure that I had not misinterpreted anything. I also asked him to do a pen sketch of himself. In the first instance he dictated this to his partner. However, she had altered it in a way John was unhappy about, so he then dictated to me and transcribed it at his IT class. This is the result:

> *My name is John. I came to Salisbury in 2001. First I lived in John Baker House which was not very nice. I got my own flat in Bournehead last June. Mary came here in August. Bournehead is a bit quiet and there isn't much to do and the last bus I can get is half three.*
>
> *I like doing things like gardening, painting-by-numbers, watching football on TV, raising money for charity, woodwork, word search, writing letters to my brother and my pen friend, helping with cooking.*
>
> *I want to go to 'Brush up your English' to learn how to spell and read and write proper so I don't have to ask other people all the time and so I can read the books and the paper and write letters better.*

Later, I arranged to visit him in his home in order to learn something of his literacy environment.

The reason John had been moved to Salisbury from the town he had lived in for most of his adult life and ultimately to Bournehead was to do with the terms of his probation. He was a convicted pædophile; the terms did not allow him to enter situations where children are present. (Towards the end of this case study, two of the contexts I looked at were made unavailable to him because the charities involved changed their constitutions to allow under 16 year olds to be involved in activities.) Due to his sensitive situation, pseudonyms are used in this account for all the people mentioned and the name of the village where he lived.

I expected to find that John was extremely isolated and finding life difficult. I already knew that he had relied heavily upon people in authority to help him with letters and forms he had received as well as to take on the role of advocate for him. He had lost all these networks. I was interested to know what he had replaced them with. This is what I learned.

John was born in 1947 in London and moved to Wiltshire with his parents and older brother when very young. His mother had died in childbirth and he was put into a children's home when he was five which he hated. At the age of seven he had moved to another children's home. From there he attended a local special school until he was 16.

John had always struggled at school finding reading and writing particularly difficult. He most enjoyed doing anything practical. He was laughed at a lot by the older boys and would try to please by helping them in some way. At 16 he was sent to residential centre in Sussex to learn how to be a painter and decorator. He was unhappy there as he got to learn little about painting and decorating and spent most of the time on chores.

In 1964 his father and his social worker moved him back to a hostel in Wiltshire and he went to work in a chicken factory. After a couple of years John moved to the town where, apart from a couple of brief periods in his life, he lived in a number of hostels for the next thirty years or so, doing menial jobs in supermarkets. His comment on this was 'I did all the jobs people don't want.' Early in 2001, he was ordered by the courts to move to Salisbury. He was no longer allowed to visit his hometown at all. This caused him distress, as everyone he knew lived in the area.

Initially, he lived in a hostel for homeless men. From the outset he disliked this intensely; the hostel was full of drinkers and drug abusers who were loud and unruly. With the help of his key worker there, he joined social centres, started to learn how to use computers at an IT centre run by a local charity and did voluntary work for other charities. He wanted to move out of the hostel; again with help from his key worker and probation officer, he found and moved into a flat in a village about six miles from Salisbury; a couple of months later, his girlfriend Mary moved to join him.

The village was small, with little on offer to occupy John. In Salisbury he got involved in various social contexts in the evenings; these were no longer available to him as the last bus from Salisbury left before 4pm. This gave little choice for an evening social life. The Parish notice board told him and Mary what was going on in the village; occasionally they would use the pub, from time to time attended church. They joined the local historical society and got involved in planning the village fête. They also attended a local 'Skills for Living' project, set up in the village by a Christian charity. John would travel to Salisbury for specific purposes, for his IT classes, to shop at the market or supermarket or to socialise at Elizabeth House.

On first visiting him in his flat, I was surprised at the amount of written material in evidence. There were newspapers, comic books, bibles, a calendar, parish newsletters, puzzle books, documentation of various sorts all organised in files. John bought *The Sun* newspaper every day and went through it from cover to cover, looking at the pictures and reading for gist; he took the local newspapers and Mary would help him read what he could not understand; he also read comic books, looking at the pictures, reading what he could of the speech bubbles and ignoring the other text. He and Mary read the Bible together because, John said, he found it too difficult to do so alone. He kept a calendar where he wrote all his appointments.

Quite often John got official letters or forms. He worried about these, because generally he could not understand them. When they arrived, he tended to try and find somebody else to help, somebody who he deemed to be in authority. In the past it would have been the staff in the hostels he had lived in. The first time I visited, it was my turn; John had been sent a form by a charity which had provided a service for him. He was being asked to give his views of the service he had received and just had to tick the correct boxes. It wasn't a complex form but because it was 'official' he wanted it to 'be right' and did not trust that he or Mary would do it justice.

John and Mary enjoyed the meetings of the local historical society and had been collecting material about the history of the area in a folder which he showed me. I asked about the minutes of the meeting which (in my view) must have been written by a wordsmith and were extremely inaccessible for people with poor literacy skills. John admitted that he found them very hard to follow when they were read out at meetings because a lot of the words were too long. Many of the other texts in this folder were far more readable for him, as they were captions to old photographs and he could work out what they said by referring to the pictures. Again, with the more complicated texts he relied on Mary.

Back in the IT classes John attended every week, there was a great deal of literacy activity going on. He very much enjoyed these, which were run with small groups of about eight people. The tutor would read out the handouts, which were simple enough for him to follow in most cases; if he got stuck, he would ask another learner. In this case the literacy practices are actually following the lesson; the events is the use of a program such as MS Word or MS Publisher to create a written document. John frequently asked the tutor to help with his spelling; if she was unavailable, he would again ask another learner.

At the weekly social club at Elizabeth House he took part in a project where members used computers to write to pen friends in an effort to improve their literacy skills, using materials from a pack which provided ideas, guides, writing frames and so on – and connections with the pen friends themselves.

John's literacy network – the people on whom he relied to help with his literacy – was narrow; mainly people he saw to be 'in authority' such as the vicar, social workers, adult education tutors – anyone who he deemed to be more able than he. Otherwise he relied on his partner, who seemed to give her help willingly. His way of reciprocating this help included: weeding the churchyard, offering to wash their cars, making tea and answering the door for the tutor of his IT class. He also helped raise money for local charities, seeing this as a way of helping where he could, as people had helped him.

Yet I was surprised in how many ways John used literacy in his day-to-day life and how adept he was at seeking (and returning) help. He enjoyed learning; in fact many of his social practices were built around learning situations.

Tony

Liz McKee

Although Tony, 51, had Irish Catholic roots, his idiolect reflected that he had always lived in the South of England. Born in Winchester, educated at a comprehensive school in Southampton, he had moved to Salisbury in the 1970s where, at the time of our meeting he was living in a Christian centre that offered support to vulnerable adults.

Perceived as lazy at school, Tony told me he had always been in the "bottom class", adding that it did not matter because he excelled at sport. Later, he had trained as a State Enrolled Nurse (SEN) and had considerable experience of working with the elderly. He said he had been able to pass the nursing exam because spelling did not matter, as long as the right words were used. Years later, living with one of his daughters, he became extremely ill with an iron overload disorder called haemochromatosis. He became too ill to work; became homeless and, eventually, moved to the care centre.

Employment in Salisbury was high, mostly in the public sector like the college, hospital, leisure and tourism and the Ministry of Defence; there was a constant influx of military personnel from all parts of the world. In recent years, 'upwardly mobile' commuters had moved to Salisbury out of London. Average wages did not keep pace with property prices and rents, contributing to severe pockets of poverty and deprivation. The care centre itself was situated in an extremely affluent location in the heart of this city, in walking distance of the cathedral and the city centre.

Tony shared some of the stereotypical characteristics of a homeless person: a middle-aged man with low self-esteem, health problems and limited literacy skills. After he became a student at Salisbury College, his tutor diagnosed him as dyslexic. This evidently caused him to feel relief. There seemed to be a valid reason for his past difficulties with literacy. While he could achieve creative and complex tasks such as writing poetry, he struggled over simple things like keeping files in order. He had always been able to read well but used to worry about writing.

Before his illness, Tony had played football; now, he went to the gym twice a week. He regularly attended literacy, numeracy, ICT and Job Search workshops at the centre as well as courses in counselling and literacy at the college. In spite of his symptoms of chronic fatigue, weakness, lethargy and impaired memory, he seemed to remain highly motivated, in the hope that improved reading and writing would enable him to get a better job.

In my interview with him, in discussions with people who knew him and from observations I was able to make of his environment, I learned something of the literacy events and practices that formed part of his life. Inspired by Mukul Saxena's account of a family's multilingual literacies, I present these now as if they had occurred in a single day (Saxena 1993: 98).

Eating his breakfast, Tony watches the news on TV. (He does not read the paper).

Next, he attends a two-hour hour Literacy and Numeracy class in the Queen Anne Room, Damascus House, where he learns about using syllables. He finishes writing a story called 'Pigged Out', using his spellmaster to check any spellings. He reads his own poem 'Tomorrow' to the class.

During the coffee break, he reads an article about Psychotherapy in the Nursing Journal.

Returning to the class, he word-processes his career history. He then meets his Key Worker, Andy, who tells him about some changes to the rules in the home. Tony reads through the job advertisements in the local newspaper. He wants to apply for the position of Support Officer at an elderly residential care home. He drafts a letter to accompany his CV; his literacy teacher will check it later.

At the college's drop-in day, he is given some advice and a college prospectus. He reads this and completes an application form to enrol for evening classes in literacy and a course in counselling.

He then takes a No. 63 bus signpost for the leisure centre. At the gym, he exercises (he is familiar with gym equipment so has no need to read the written instructions explaining its use). In the supermarket he buys a drink and picks up a leaflet on 'healthy eating' to read later.

Back at the care centre, he completes a DHSS form. He has few problems form filling, but he will ask Andy to check it. Later, with Judy, he goes to the session of the counselling course at the college. There, he has to prepare a five-minute presentation about himself and is given a brief outline of the course.

In the evening, on his way to the literacy class, he stops to read different notices. Once there, he listens to (and watches) another member of the group giving a Powerpoint presentation on Salisbury Cathedral. He asks questions about it, noting similarities with Winchester. He has written several pages for his own presentation on the brewery where he used to work. With the help of another learner, he surfs the net to try and find some pictures.

After the class, he meets his friends Sheila and Eileen who are former colleagues from the hospital and Peter, an old football associate. At home, he writes his reflective journal for the counselling course and a profile of himself for his literacy teacher. He prepares a rough draft first and then rewrites it, trying to scan the text for any mistakes. It takes a long time as he uses the dictionary to check spellings and the thesaurus to try and find some different words that he can use. He reads over the work and learns some spellings by repetition. He reads a chapter from a book about self-hypnosis; he would like to have a go himself one day.

Tony had extensive kin ties (mostly female) and strong associations with the local community. In his former marriage, his wife had handled the paperwork. In his nursing career, he found written work he could copy and the Nursing Officer checked his essays. At Damascus House, he had a dense network to whom he could turn for the role of literacy broker. Having spent much of his life avoiding literacy, his literacy practices had been embedded in his culture over many years and he had developed coping strategies that were part of his social networks. As a result of serious illness, these networks had become disrupted and Tony had to find alternative strategies. In returning to formal education and training, he had developed independent solutions to his dyslexia-associated problems and, in effect, learned new literacies. He seemed to have become more confident in writing, and through this, able to make some constructive changes in his life. As he put it: 'All the literacy in the world does not really mean anything. You have got to go and do it.'

His mind, he felt, worked faster than he could write; it had frustrated him that he was unable to put on paper what was in his mind. Since attending adult literacy classes he had found that there were many people worse than him and this had given him confidence. He found that he had developed a desire to know more; now that he wrote daily, he could see the improvements. For the first time in his life, he was enjoying writing.

Syl

Haoli Rein

In the process of collecting stories and examples of her literacy activities, Syl and I both became increasingly aware of the multitude of literacy events that she entered into every day. We then looked at some of them more closely to determine (a) their purpose and register and (b) the response they produced in Syl and how they made her feel about herself and her surroundings. By taking her personal context (her daily routine, surroundings, social networks she partakes in etc.) into account, we started to realise how her context and her literacy events were interwoven.

Syl had come to England from Hungary just over two years before, at the age of 26, with the intention of improving her English and thereby her job prospects in her country's developing role in the world of international business. Her visa had only allowed her to work in a temporary capacity in a position which would not further her career, but this condition suited her, as she wanted to mix with people at 'grass roots level' where she would pick up the vernacular and thereby learn the 'language of the people.'

During this two-year period however, instead of returning to her home country, she met and married an Englishman. Suddenly her need to speak, read and write the English language, took on a whole new purpose and perspective.

One of her first challenges was to find work; she got a job as a supermarket checkout operator (rather different to her work as a supervisor in Hungary). Although her spoken English was good, she could think more quickly in her new 'home language' than she could speak or write it. In the self-portrait she wrote for me, this is how she chose to describe her life, her interests and her aspirations:

> *My name is Syl. I'm 28 years old. I live in Swindon. I'm married to a super man. I'm lucky. I always wanted to be able to speak English fluently. (My mother tongue is Hungarian). I've done it. I love to travel.*

> *I've done a lot. Now I'm studying IT at New College and hopefully I will be able to work with computers after I've finished my courses.*

> *I would like to design Web pages. It is very important to speak and write fluently because I want to get a good job.*

> *I'm very busy every day. I go to the college in the mornings, I leave from there at 12 o'clock, start to work in Asda at 1 o'clock. Such a rush. I'm a checkout operator. I finish the work at 9 o'clock. After I got home I start to cook something quickly. Bathtime and bedtime. GONE ...*

Syl and her husband lived in a semi-detached house on a typical middle-income estate in Swindon. Her neighbours were mostly young professionals who drove fairly new cars, wore fashionable clothes, frequented the local gym and took holidays in far-flung places. Syl told me that when she conversed with her neighbours, she was keenly aware of what she felt to be her 'socially unaccept-able accent.' ('Why unacceptable?' one may ask. After several months of customers commenting on the way she spoke and asking her to repeat herself at the supermarket, this was the conclusion she had come to. Her name – spelt 'Szil' in Hungarian – had also drawn attention and, after having to explain herself over and over again and deal with her own frustration, she had asked to have her name-badge changed to the English 'Syl' instead.)

It was an environment which encouraged consumption. Syl was bombarded daily with the perception of an 'ideal life' as portrayed by English culture through the lifestyle of her neighbours, magazines, television, radio, the gym etc. She and her husband, however, were working hard to become financially secure, so when offers for credit came through the letterbox, she had to resist the enticing offers of low interest rates. Instead, she concentrated on the specials offered through pamphlets, and television and the discount she could get at Asda. She wrote: 'I love to travel', and by watching out for specials on flights, she and her husband had been able to book a trip to Spain in the summer, having waded through the piles of holiday brochures adorning her lounge table and searching the internet. (She told me that the hours of reading were going to pay dividends when she returned 'brown as a berry').

Having read about literacy events and practices, I set out, with Syl, to discover how various areas of her life – her home, college life and work-place – were affected by the literacy events, practices and registers she encountered. Without even leaving the confines of her home, we found a good range, with varying ideological preconceptions underpinning them. These are two examples.

One of the first areas we looked at was that of food. Syl was used to a different diet to her husband, but David worked hard at a local factory, often doing shift work. She held to the 'folk model' that as his wife, she needed to send him off with 'a full tummy' so that he could concentrate on his work and not on his hunger. She kept her own recipes for weekends, giving him during the week the food he was most used to. One of his favourites was 'Poor Man's Pudding.' This entailed Syl having to interpret his Mother's recipe whilst working within the informal register (as defined by Yule 1996, p 244), of 'tried and trusted' food literacies.

In stark contrast was the official register of the documents she had to deal with in applying for 'Indefinite Leave to Remain' in the UK. This involved a lengthy application, in which she had to prove to 'the authorities' that, among other things, she was still married and employed and that she had not had to depend in any way on 'public funds.' To do this, she not only had to contend with legal terminology, but also with the knowledge that 'the powers that be' had the authority to say no. While this was unlikely in her case, as she was married to a British citizen, compiling such an application caused her some tension and anxiety. David was very helpful however, and while she was a very independent young woman, she appreciated his support with more involved literacy events such as this.

Other registers she encountered included those of instruction and advertising. Using her new washing machine meant having to work through the instructions, and searching for better employment meant she had to wade through the advertisements found in jobseekers newspapers such as 'Jobs & Careers.' To find another position, she had to be able to understand the register of the working world – including terms such as 'team player' and 'able to use initiative' – and then be able to present herself in a professional manner by means of a literacy practice of some importance – writing her CV.

Most of Syl's networks were uniplex, the only dense ones being between herself, her husband and her husband's family. Among her college associates, the literacy practices were purposeful in that everyone was aiming to improve their computer literacy or their English and in her case, to acquire a better job. At work, she needed to know where products were kept and be able to identify them quickly when pricing items at the checkout, in order to be able to respond quickly to customer needs.

While additional dense networks might have helped Syl feel more 'at home', the varied environments in which she operated resulted in her hearing many different registers which in turn, increased her linguistic repertoire and helped her to integrate into her new-found cultural environment.

In looking at these different aspects of Syl's life, we realised that the social environment in which she lived played a vital role in how she interpreted the texts which she encountered on a daily basis – and how they in turn, affect her perspective on her environment.

Syl is, of course, only one learner, but having worked along side her in this quest for insight into the world of literacy events, I felt I could agree that literacy *is* best understood as 'a set of social practices' and that we need 'to recognise the central role of power relations' in them (Street 1993: 2). So saying, this whole exercise opened not only Syl's eyes to the world of literacy events and practices which she encounters almost every waking moment of the day – but also my own.

Martin

Mig Holder

In setting out to investigate the literacy practices of one particular learner, I tried to start with as open a mind as possible, free of preconceptions both about the person or the outcomes I would discover. In the event, what emerged was interesting in two distinct ways:

> *a striking before and after scenario for this learner, caused by a major life trauma; and*

> *a challenge to not only my, but our, (literacy teachers, policy makers and politicians') assumptions about the reasons people attend literacy classes, their motivation and their 'barriers to learning'*

'Martin' (not his real name, though he was willing for me to use it), had been a student in my Literacy and Creative Writing classes for about a term and I often saw him around college. Even so, I knew very few of the facts, set out below, that he was willing to share with me, and that have so markedly affected his life in the past eight years.

Knowing that I am a fairly strong character and that he might feel he had to say particular things to 'please' me as the teacher, I chose not to start our main discussions until he had completed a short piece of writing about himself. The shape of the investigation was therefore as follows:

1. Explaining the project to Martin and getting his agreement

2. Asking him to write a piece about himself and the literacy in his life

3. Extended discussion around his background, education, family life

4. Presenting the outline information to our seminar group

5. Having a further discussion with Martin, focusing on some of the specifically literacy-related issues raised by the group.

I had been worried about being able to record accurately what Martin said to me in discussion while still maintaining eye contact and rapport with him. In the event this was 'aided' by Martin's severe stammer, which meant that he talked quite slowly, and I felt that my looking down to write from time to time actually took the pressure off him.

Born in 1953, he had been brought up in a close-knit industrial community in Derbyshire. His father was the managing director of a company making car seats for Jaguar and Triumph. The family had a good standard of living; his parents were supportive of his schooling (in 'convent' schools and the local secondary modern school.) He recalled his school experience as 'confined':

> *For instance, we were taught Mary Queen of Scots was good because she was Catholic. It's true, it's a fact. It was very strict, indoctrinated, very sheltered.*

He had not disliked school; in fact, he said, he had enjoyed English, Maths, history and geography. When asked if he found English easy to do, he replied 'if I was interested'; then, as an afterthought:

> *except reading out loud, because of my stammer ...in those days you had to stand up and read out a bit of Tom Sawyer or Animal Farm ... I used to dread that lesson. Kids are very cruel.*

He developed skills in woodwork, metal work and technical drawing and after training as a chef at a college in Manchester, he went on to work for six years in the catering trade. It was at this time, he said, that he got into a drinking habit.

The community in Derbyshire was very traditional. Martin did not like it as it was:

> *too regimented, everyone knows everyone else's business. The same "pub-team" propping up the bar every week.*

With his wife and two children, he achieved a council house exchange and moved to Weston-super-Mare. Everything went well until, in 1996, he was involved in an horrific accident at work, falling off a broken ladder, which left him with appalling injuries to his leg and the effects of a severe blow to the head. He was in hospital for nine months out of the next two years, having 14 operations and being confined to a wheelchair for long periods.

The firm Martin had been working for admitted liability and this proved to be his downfall:

> *Because it was their fault, they gave me a pension as if I'd worked there for forty years, and a third of a million pounds compensation. I had all the time in the world, nothing to do, and money coming out of my ears.*

He then started drinking heavily and became an alcoholic:

> *I was hiding drink in the greenhouse, in the garden – one big deceit – my wife didn't know; she thought I was in the first stages of Alzheimers.*

Seven miserable years and an attempted suicide later, Martin stopped drinking and came to college, at his wife's suggestion, to 'keep himself occupied'. At the time of our work on this project, he was attending classes in English, maths, IT and local history, (with 'embedded' basic skills), for a large part of the week. He would be seen around college all the time, at lessons and workshops, using the computers, and generally socialising. He looked totally at home and told me:

> *I'm more happier now than I've ever been.*

I invited Martin to talk about the part that reading, writing and speaking had played in his life, both before and after the accident. As I have already indicated, he had no specific issues when it came to writing, except as part of his general satisfaction at his learning programme; and apart from the cruel reactions to his pronounced stammer, he had taken no particular anxieties or stigma around his literacy from his school life. As a young married man he had been part of the close-knit community where the accepted norm was for the men to be the breadwinners and the women to look after the household business and the children.

> *You didn't need to – it was that kind of culture – good enough for your father and grandfather? It's good enough for you. Usually it was the wives did money and letters and that sort of thing. She's always been very academic, my wife, anyway.*

This role differentiation is in marked contrast to that described by Barton and Padmore (1994) in the community they researched, where, even in cases where the male partner had poorer literacy and numeracy skills, he was still involved in domestic business and especially the paying of bills. In Martin's case this distribution of tasks continued after the move to Weston-super-Mare,

> *My wife has always done the paperwork at home – I was always happy for*

her to. I didn't do much with the kids homework etc – I was very happy keeping the wolf from the door. But [referring to the accident] it was all taken away from me in one swoop.

The picture that seemed to be emerging very much contradicts the one that we so often see cited in the conventional wisdom of adult basic skills. Neither in Derbyshire nor in Weston-super-Mare had Martin's lack of involvement or skill with literacy or numeracy affected him adversely, in his words:

I never bothered about filling in forms, tax returns etc.

and

If I didn't know a word, I'd just ask somebody – it didn't bother me.

It was after his accident, as Martin went on to explain, that there was a shift in the balance of responsibilities, which in turn had complex effects.

When I came out of hospital, I'd become institutionalised – everything was done for me – I didn't have to worry about bills or anything. It was so strange with me not being the breadwinner. It made me feel inferior.

At this point, again in contrast to some common assumptions, this shift in balance between the partners did not itself motivate Martin to improve his basic skills. In his case it wasn't the lack of literacy skills or involvement in literacy events that caused the feelings of inferiority; it was much more the change in balance of 'power' in the relationship caused by his not being able to work. The self-esteem issues here are much more complex than a simple causal relationship between who 'does the books' and what they feel about it.

When I asked Martin who now looked after the household finances and correspondence he replied:

Even now if you was to ask me how much we got in the bank account, I wouldn't have a clue … I don't write letters – the only letters I've wrote are college work!

Despite his new-found pleasure and skill in literacy and numeracy, he still did not feel the need to boost his sense of identity or self-esteem by involving himself in the family paperwork.

We talked about reading for pleasure. Martin said that this had figured very little in his life until recently:

In thirty-five years I'd only read the sports pages and that kind of thing. To sit down and read a book wouldn't have entered my head.

While this had certainly changed since he had been coming to literacy classes, this reading was very much related to his college work.

> *Now at home I'm reading and writing all the time – mainly college work and reading books – like more sports books now. I think more than anything I like doing projects – learning how to do the index, the bibliography with start middle and an end.*

At the same time, there was clearly a pleasure in this kind of reading: a pleasure which had become associated, for him, with another:

> *If I'm honest, when I started college, I was using it to my own ends – I was occupied all day. But within a month of starting, that all went. I just enjoy learning.*

The more Martin shared his thoughts with me, the more his story broke the stereotype of an adult literacy learner. However hard I 'pushed' him, there was no evidence that he had identified a *functional* need to improve his literacy or that poor literacy skills per se were the cause of any lack of self-esteem. Policy writing over the years assumes that people with lower levels of basic skills have a poor educational background, lack of parental support and a sense of stigma in having someone else to do their paperwork and so on. In Martin's case, all these bit the dust. His relationship with literacy was more complex. In his writing and interviews, he referred much more to changing his life and learning to learn than to 'improving his English'. It was also inseparable from the other strands of his new sense of worth – learning, being sober, being a new person.

> *It's like, without trying to sound soppy, it's like I've found a new me since I haven't had a drink.*

I believe that, as literacy practitioners, we need to hear this complexity.

Commentary

Almost half of Sheila Nicholson's account of Jed's life, interests and literacy activities, consists of her commentary on these findings in relation to general views of literacy and a close set of connections with theoretical writing, concluding with a concern about the limits of this kind of study

Susan portrays John as a man whose life was circumscribed by the conditions of a probation order. In her account of the research process, she reminds us of the sometimes awkward relationship between scribe and author (Mace 2002), with John's partner wanting to alter the pensketch of himself that he dictated to her. She also tells us of the surprise available to a researcher who is open to unexpected findings: she had not expected to see John as someone using literacy so often and strategically in his everyday life.

In presenting her findings, Liz McKee has taken inspiration from Mukul Saxena's ethnographic study of Punjabi literacies in a west London community: assembling in an imaginary single day the literacy events that Tony undertakes on a regular basis. The picture is of necessity artificial, making Tony's day look very full of literacy indeed. What is interesting is how the educational settings feature in a flow of other scenes in which Tony uses reading and writing.

The process of the research which Haoli Rein undertook with Syl is presented as a partnership. As Haoli saw it, during their discussions about Syl's literacy interests and activities, they both grew in awareness. We would need Syl's comment on the process to know whether she saw it that way too: but certainly the combination of pen portrait, meeting in the home and their collaborative study of her literacy events around cooking and immigration help us imagine that she might well have done.

In the last of this section, we find more of the subject's spoken words than in any previous piece. There are always practical problems to be overcome in recording verbatim utterances and Mig refers to the possible tensions of simultaneously interviewing and transcribing the words of the interviewee. In this case, Martin's slight speech impediment worked in her favour and she felt her pauses to scribble gave him a welcome pause from interaction. The result of her efforts is very much more of the subject's own words than we have found in other reports. It gives us something more of his personality than we can gain from the third-person report, with his particular rhythm and idioms.

Chapter 5

Research informing practice

Ellayne Fowler

This project began as an aspect of teacher training. That is what we come back to in this final chapter. How do we carry into teaching the perspective we have outlined in this book?

Brian Street warns that there is no direct link between theory and practice (2003: 84) and Wenger makes the same point:

> A perspective is not a recipe: it does not tell you just what to do. Rather it acts as a guide about what to pay attention to, what difficulties to expect, and how to approach problems. (Wenger 1998:9)

In this chapter we are going to suggest some areas that we, as teachers, need to pay attention to, while highlighting potential problems and suggesting ways of overcoming them. Nothing we suggest is totally new; rather it is a way of approaching teaching holistically.

A social practice perspective on adult literacy

What, then, should we 'pay attention to'? Geraldine Castleton takes up Brian Street's call for literacy provision to focus on 'change':

> If the focus is put on 'change', that is, how people can and want to use literacy to bring about change in their lives, then literacy, and consequently the people looking for support, can be viewed in a far more positive light … Such a framing allows for recognition of the ways in which people use literacy as a resource shared by members of communities of practice in which participants assume different roles for different purposes. (Castleton 2001: 66).

If we focus on 'change' we get a different framework for assessing, planning and delivering adult literacy teaching. It begins by acknowledging what students do, how they use literacy and how they need support in order to accomplish change in their lives. It positions the learner as a member of different communities of practice, as we all are. It acknowledges what the learner brings to learning in contrast to a deficit model, which positions the learner in terms of the skills that he lacks.

A social practice view of education is a powerful thing, because it acknowledges learning as participation, wherever that takes place. Wenger clarifies that participation is not simply in an educational context:

> Participation here refers not just to local events of engagement in certain activities with certain people, but to a more encompassing process of being active participants in the practices of social communities and constructing identities in relation to these communities ... Such participation shapes not only what we do, but also who we are and how we interpret what we do. (Wenger 1989: 4)

What these learner profiles illustrate is how participation in various communities of practice results in change. As Mig Holder writes about Martin in Chapter 4, 'He referred much more to changing his life and learning to learn than to *improving his English*'. Learners' lives change in terms of:

- the literacy practices they use

- the roles they play in particular communities of practice

- their sense of identity

- the communities of practice in which they participate in.

We should also say at this point that *learner* in this case encompasses both basic skills learner and trainee teacher.

Changing literacy practices

An examination of how literacy practices change necessarily looks beyond the acquisition of new skills in the classroom. It has to encompass how practices change or are transferred to different settings, as well as the values that are attached to those practices.

A change in literacy practices may come through joining a new community of practice or a changing role in an existing one. Jed (Chapter 4) illustrates this in his workplace practices. When Jed had to take on the role of a silver service waiter he had to learn to take down people's orders, which was a new literacy event. He managed this by looking over people's shoulders at the menu. That literacy event then translates into a new practice for Jed that he learned by participating in the social activity. He used a strategy that he had developed in other contexts. No one had taught him how to do this: as he had put it, 'Work is always teaching me.'

While Jed illustrates learning through participation, other profiles illustrate how difficult it can be for people to transfer practices from one setting to another, which has direct implications for classroom teaching. Marie Anne (Chapter 1), for example, 'regularly wrote long and newsy letters to her pen friends; yet in the class she had considerable difficulty composing informal letters'. This led her teacher, Kauser McCallum to wonder if she was 'describing the person she wanted to be and the skills to which she aspired rather than those she actually possessed'. What Kauser discovered was that Marie Anne had an efficient method for composing informal letters to pen friends that involved her sending a draft to her friend Diane, discussion over the phone and then rewriting. In this case the setting of the classroom disrupted the vernacular literacy practice of writing an informal letter, as it didn't obviously provide the supportive network that enabled the vernacular practice.

This could be traced to the value that Marie Anne attached to literacy in the classroom (perhaps it should be error free). It could be because the teacher cannot replace the friend as literacy mediator (is there some judgement involved in the teacher's feedback? This may not be the case, but could be the expectation of a student who associates classroom literacy with previous experience). However, without exploring Marie Anne's literacy practices around letter writing, the teacher can end up with a picture of her shortcomings rather than strengths and Marie Anne might have difficulty working on the skills that would make her letter writing more independent. This also argues for breaking down the barriers between classroom and vernacular literacies. While students see classroom literacy as something 'other' than what they do, there is little chance for them to value the practices they already have and can build on.

In looking at literacy as social practice, we are exploring the values people attach to and their attitudes towards these different practices. If we don't do this as teachers, we can jump to the wrong conclusions about people's abilities. Michael (Chapter 3) was unable to find information from a picture of a sign in a car park. This can be interpreted as an inability to infer meaning. However, if we tie this to Michael's attitude to reading – 'He would not consider reading for pleasure; to him it was a learning tool' – we might interpret it differently. Michael would not look for information in print. He might have asked someone he saw in the car park if he could park there for free on Sundays, but print was not a source of information for him. For Michael literacy was something that happens in the classroom.

It is not just the classroom setting that can limit the use of literacy practices. The case of Chris (Chapter 3) illustrates how important setting can be for literacy practices. He was able to partake in a group reading of the newspaper in one setting, but not in another. His inability to transfer this practice was tied up to his sense of identity and how people see him. In a familiar setting, where he was known, he felt able to take part. In the new community of practice his difficulties with reading became a barrier to participation because of how he felt he would be judged.

For the teachers involved in this research, exploring literacy practices with their students raised their own awareness. Gill Whalley wrote:

> *The research reinforced and brought alive for me the reality of seeing literacy as a practice which is always socially situated. As a teacher I am much more aware of, and interested in, the different role literacy practices play in learners' real lives and the social meaning such practices carry.*

Changing roles

We all take on many roles in the communities of practice we belong to. (Today I have been mum, academic writer, teacher, friend, party organiser, wife, and it's not lunchtime yet.) This research focused participants on the roles they play, as teachers, in their learners' lives and the roles that learners take in their own networks. These roles are often valued and independent of literacy ability and they can change. The consequences of that change also became clear.

One of the striking findings in looking at the research as a whole, was how many teachers realised they had become a part of their learner's social network and thereby had a role in it. This was often as a literacy expert who was independent of the student's other social networks. For Dave (Chapter 1) 'his tutor was someone independent whom he could trust to help him'. Susan Buchanan became someone in authority for John (Chapter 4) to turn to in dealing with the official literacy in his life. Moreover, the classroom can offer a network that is independent of the other networks in a person's life. For Jed (Chapter 4), who would normally ask his family for help, the adult literacy group provided independent support for completing a form: 'the college had become part of his network, a place where he could fill in forms as part of his work during the lesson, with the support of a tutor.' Sheila Nicholson links this with Jed's wish to be independent.

While the tutor can become part of the learner's social network, learner and teacher do not always maintain the same roles in that network. Jackie Winch-combe shows how Rachel (Chapter 3) and she changed roles when considering knitting patterns:

> *In this literacy practice I was less literate than Rachel because although I could read the words on the knitting pattern they had little or no meaning for me.*

In this case, as often happens when learners share their expertise, the teacher becomes the novice and the learner the expert.

This is not an isolated example of changing roles within social networks. Perhaps it is only when the spotlight is on literacy problems that we fail to see how asking an experienced person for help and then offering our own help as we gain experience is a normal part of our social life. Consider, for example, Gillian Knox's portrait of Joyce, who had sought help from a disabled friend to fill in disability forms:

She viewed the process as a partnership, we puzzle it out together, and the friend completed the blank spaces with the agreed response to the question.

Joyce's friend had had to deal with these forms before and was therefore experienced. Gillian notes at the end of the profile that:

Her experience of filling in the disability benefit form had also given her the confidence to advise another neighbour about his disability allowance.

Joyce, a novice, had now gained expertise. We play many roles within our own communities of practice. We are not either expert or novice, but swap roles depending on the context we find ourselves in. So while Irene (Chapter 3) might get help with her spelling from other nuns on one day, on another she would be helping them with their Christmas letter writing:

She helped them with the "thinking" – getting ideas for the letters – while they did the actual scribing themselves.

What these changing roles highlight again is Arlene Fingeret's notion of reciprocity, for, as she says, 'Social networks operate on the basis of mutual exchange' (1983:136).

Fingeret identifies a risk attached to learning to read and write for the adults in her study, that 'they may become alienated from network members and subcultural conventions' (*ibid.*:144). We saw this in the profile of Pauline (Chapter 2), who had competed a tax form without her husband's help, which led to him being 'quite huffy' with her, imagining she no longer needed his help. As Karen Bilous points out:

It was as if there had been an unspoken agreement in the marriage, by which he was made happy when he was able to do things that she was unable to do for herself. Now that she was emerging and taking control of her literacy the power balance had changed.

Fingeret takes up this potential difficulty in her advice to teachers:

Educators must become involved in the social networks of illiterate adults and must recognize that the development of literacy skills, even for one individual, entails a broader process of social change. (1983:145)

While the teachers in this project recognized their roles in learner's social networks it is important to also realise how an adult literacy process can have other consequences in existing networks.

One of the most positive things that we learn from this research is how many of the learners have valued roles in their communities that aren't tied to their literacy skills at all. We have already revisited Irene, who was elected Abbess during her time in the basic skills class. Pauline, who according to national standards was functionally illiterate, had been chairperson of the local playgroup, where she was known as a 'good delegater'. Sam (Chapter 2) was highly valued in his wide-ranging networks, for his organisational skills which did not rely on literacy. Clare Griffin echoed the sentiments of others when, giving her feedback after the project, she wrote that the research, 'reinforced the importance of not making assumptions about learners and how much our learners deserve our respect.'

Changing identity

One theme that emerges from many of the profiles concerns the learner's sense of identity in relation to literacy tasks. Wenger emphasises identity as one of the four components of learning. He writes of it as, 'a way of talking about how learning changes who we are and creates personal histories of becoming in the context of our communities' (1998: 5). How does learning change our identity? Think of learning to drive, for example. When you start (as we mentioned in the introduction) you are a *learner*. Then when you pass your test you become a *driver*, although this often qualified – *a new driver, a probationary driver*. As you gain experience you become an *experienced driver* or you can take another test to become an *advanced driver*. This exemplifies how identity is about learning as becoming. Many of the learners involved in this project saw their lack of literacy skills reflected in other people's perceptions of them and the labels that were attached to them. Part of their learning purpose could be expressed as a wish to become *differently literate*.

Jed (Chapter 4) was not embarrassed by his lack of literacy skills; on the contrary, as Sheila Nicholson relates, 'he was proud of assuming responsibility for his own learning.' However, he did want 'to shake off the special needs mantle that had always surrounded him.' In a similar vein, John (Chapter 1) was still very embarrassed about having gone 'to a special school, known locally as the *backward* school.' As Chris Topham writes, 'Once he became proficient at writing, he hoped to show his family that he could be independent and should be treated with greater respect.' It can take a long time to achieve a new sense of identity, losing labels you have acquired along the way.

Not all labels are negative. For Tony (Chapter 4) being told he was dyslexic was a relief as 'there seemed to be a valid reason for his past difficulties with literacy.' This is not always the case though, as Vicky (Chapter 3) illustrates. She restricted the people who knew about her dyslexia to a 'need to know basis'. Perhaps the difference was that Vicky had been diagnosed at school. Where the label of dyslexic came as a relief to Tony after years of problems, for Vicky it had been part of how she was seen from a young age. How people see us forms part of our identity and goes some way to explaining the lengths that people will go to hide literacy difficulties in a society where literacy is judged to be important.

Another element of identity is cultural. We think of ourselves as British or English or Jamaican or European. This label reflects cultural communities that we feel we belong to. Moze (Chapter 2) illustrates how a change of cultural setting can have an adverse effect on sense of identity. Mandy Weatherett writes of her:

> *In Israel, Moze's command of The English language was considered an asset and her fluency was admired by both English and Hebrew speakers. American English had a powerful influence and Moze had mastered it so well that she was able to convince strangers that she was Hispanic American.*

However in England this changed.

> *Moze now worked on a deficit model of literacy, as she was often judged, and certainly feared being judged, by her inabilities rather than her abilities.*

Moze's abilities are not different, but the context against which they are judged has changed.

What this research seems to have done for the learners involved, as reported by the teachers, is to have resulted in improved self-confidence. Eight out of eleven authors responding to an email we sent round reported this. Tricia Jones told us that Sarah's confidence and enthusiasm had been so enhanced she won an award in Adult Learners' Week. In discussing the process of research (Chapter 4) we saw how Gillian Knox had found her subject to be less worried about her intruding on her privacy than Gillian had thought she would be. We also saw how Gillian shared the 'criteria' of the project with Joyce. One of the outcomes of this sense of shared process, as Gillian discovered it, was that Joyce recognised that she was more active and capable than she had thought herself to be. This is someone who had fully absorbed the deficit view of her own abilities, for whom the social practice view of her literacy life had shed a different light on them:

> *I don't think she had ever considered that she may be 'good' at anything – she had only centred on her literacy difficulties. Seeing her capabilities and achievements recorded in print certainly gave her self-esteem a boost.*

Gill Whalley reported that, 'Chris's confidence and self image as a learner definitely strengthened and he valued the fact he was helping me with my work'. This reciprocity reflects the reciprocity found by so many of the researchers in the social networks of learners. As Arlene Fingeret wrote of her study, 'I asked these adults if they would teach me about their lives and, once they agreed, many of them took this responsibility very seriously' (1983: 134). This research process allowed teacher and learner to change roles and allowed learners to acknowledge the vernacular literacy practices in their lives as literacy, with a perceived effect on their own self worth.

Changing communities of practice

The student profiles illustrate how changing communities of practice can have an effect on someone's sense of identity and lead to them attending an Adult Literacy class. The profiles also demonstrate communities of practice that are based very much on the written word, such as the army, the convent and education. While the educational community of practice can often lead to feelings of inadequacy in terms of literacy skills, it can also be liberating.

A number of profiles demonstrate how joining a new community of practice can change perception of skills levels. We have already seen how Chris (Chapter 3) was unable to participate in the same literacy event he was comfortable with in his social club within his new community of practice in the workplace. Ruth (Chapter 2) is another person who behaved differently in different communities. Within her family she received a lot of literacy support from her grown up children, reciprocating with support for her grandchildren's literacy. However, in her church community she felt unable to share her difficulties with literacy. Clare Griffin tells us:

> *This inability to admit her lack of literacy to the church elders seems to be clearly linked to the power relations between church and congregation, teacher and pupil.*

It is perhaps also linked to Ruth's sense of identity and how she wants people to see her. What was driving her need to change was the wish to evangelise. In order to do this she would have to attend Bible college, which entails a whole range of literacy practices that she needed to develop.

For others, entry into a new community of practice had profound effects on their self-image. Pauline, for example, had been successfully employed and had partaken in community events. However, as Karen Bilous writes:

> *Pauline's life (and literacies) changed radically after she joined the local Evangelical church … In our interview Pauline stated that she had not really missed being able to read until she had started to attend the bible reading group.*

Pauline's learning story is one of success. She joined a basic skills group and is now able to participate in a number of literacy events connected to the church. Karen points out though,

> *At the same time, it seems from my interview with her that Pauline had*

begun to feel a lesser person when in a situation where she compared her lack of reading and writing skills with others ...

The need to improve skills was motivated by a change to a community of practice that relied on the written word.

We have seen other examples of this sort of community of practice in the portraits in this book. Irene (Chapter 3) allows us a glimpse into another religious community, already mentioned above, which is also based on the text of the Bible. Michael, in the same chapter, allows us a glimpse into army life. Sue Thain interviewed a soldier, who told her,

... it is written down. How to do a patrol, how to bed down for the night, what to do when you get fired at. It's all there in black and white.

Another community of practice that relies on the written word would be education. Adult literacy teachers who work within a standardised system must often feel they write more than their learners in terms of assessment, target setting and reviews in order to prove learner progress and, ultimately, value for government money. Where someone has moved to such a community of practice it is easy to see how they then have a need to develop literacy practices to move from the margins into the centre of that community.

Motivation for change

In considering learning as change, we have suggested themes that we need to pay attention to as teachers:

- looking at literacy practices rather than concentrating solely on skills

- awareness of roles taken, for both teacher and learner and how taking a new role in a community can have unsettling effects on other members of that network

- understanding how a learner's sense of identity changes through learning and the positive and negative effects that can have for them

- understanding literacy practices within the context of communities of practice and how movement between these communities affects learner needs in terms of literacy practices.

It is also worth at this point expanding on this last point. What is the motivation for change that brings a learner to the classroom? The drive to improve national literacy standards is often functional, in terms of improving the nation's economy through upgrading workers' skills. However, *The Adult Literacy Core Curriculum* for England makes clear that this should be used in conjunction with the learner's context, which can be classified under the following headings:

Citizen and community

Economic activity, including paid and unpaid work

Domestic and everyday life

Leisure

Education and training

Using ICT in social roles

(BSA 2001)

What these profiles have shown is how the motivation for change comes from across this range of contexts. It may be linked to economic activity. Dave (Chapter 1) had suffered economic consequences because of his lack of literacy skills while working for Tesco. He started in the fresh produce team, but, as Sarah Lyster writes,

> *He had great difficulty reading the labels and so was moved the back door where the goods were delivered.*

And so Dave came into an adult literacy class through the support of a manager at work.

Education and training are at the forefront for Sarah (Chapter 1) who wanted to be a florist. She needed to develop academic literacy practices to enable her to train. Vicky (Chapter 3) really wanted to 'sit in the park on a sunny day, with a can of lager and read the paper'. Her motivation could be classed as leisure. Rachel (Chapter 3) and Martin (Chapter 4) seem to have primarily social reasons for attending classes, with Martin coming to college to 'keep himself occupied.'

Teachers, in their feedback following this research, wrote about how it had helped them explore more both the learner as an individual and their social context. For Claire Griffin, the work 'reinforced the importance of not making assumptions about learners'. The value of visiting something of the learner's life and context could shed a new light on their interests in classroom learning. Kate Tomlinson wrote: 'I felt I knew about Irene, but this gave me a rounder, broader picture of her.' Knowledge about what the learner does outside the classroom is not just a resource for the teacher, but can also be a resource for the group. As Sheila Nicholson pointed out, it's not just about finding out about the learner's literacy needs: 'It may be that they have experiences and interests which they could be encouraged to share to enrich the learning experiences of others'.

Implications for the teaching process

When considering the implications for literacy research and practice of the social practice view of literacy, Brian Street suggests these should be based on a number of principles. He begins with, 'Literacy is more complex than current curriculum and assessment allows' (2003: 84). This was echoed in comments from the teachers involved in this project. Gill Whalley wrote, for example:

> *The case study reinforced for me that rather than focusing on learners' 'needs' and 'deficits', we need to refocus on how complex and sophisticated communication skills actually are.*

Literacy skills exist and can be listed in a curriculum, but they don't exist in a vacuum. They are embedded in social practices. To explore the implications of this way of looking at literacy we will look at stages in the teaching process in order to explore how our practice might take this view into account. This is not a blueprint for teaching, although it does contain some practical ideas. At this point in time, it is a call for further work by teachers and learners in adult literacy classes to try this out, to develop materials and to share practice with others. The practical suggestions have been used in an adult literacy class.

Assessment

Current practice in England suggests that assessment can be split into distinct stages – screening, initial, diagnostic – although reality suggests these often overlap in initial interviews with potential students. The use of the term *diagnostic* suggests a medical discourse that pinpoints a medical difficulty or illness. Further reading of the English diagnostic assessment materials (DfES publications) suggests a more even approach that acknowledges student strengths as well as weaknesses. However, in order to fully take on the social practices view of literacy, assessment should do more than measure the skills someone possesses.

Brian Street argues that teaching 'has to be able to take account of the variation in literacy practices amongst students' and to give value to home literacies (*ibid.*: 85). We would also argue that assessment needs to record how people use literacy. It was only through these case studies that learners and teachers acknowledged what learners were already able to do. An assessment that measures an educational literacy practice in terms of skills privileges a certain type of literacy. Exploring what learners did improved their self-esteem and, as Street points out:

> from a pedagogic point of view, what is there to be built upon if the aim is to help such people to add dominant literacy practices to their linguistic repertoire? (ibid.: 81).

Practical idea 1

You have ten learners in your classroom and can't possibly do a case study on each of them. What you can do though is explore literacy practices in group discussion around specific topics.

- **What do people read?** Bring in lots of examples of junk mail, magazines, papers, website pages, maps, timetables to act as models. Explore reading as something that isn't just about books and understanding dense text. Ask people to bring in something they have read for the next session and ask them to talk about it. This begins to bring vernacular literacy practices into the classroom and foregrounds the everyday. It can also illuminate learner interests of which you were unaware.

- **What letters do people actually write?** This discussion may bring out very few examples of letters, but can uncover interesting uses of text and e-mail, which seem to be replacing letter writing, except in very formal contexts. This in turn, may lead to an informed and lively discussion of the level of formality of language that was appropriate to these different formats.

This more rounded view of assessment has an effect on any targets set for a student. For targets to be truly SMART (Specific, Measurable, Achievable, Realistic and Time-bound) they should link skills to practices. Picking up on our example of letter writing, the student should not simply produce a letter in the classroom, but send it to someone.

Teaching

While acknowledging that theory does not directly translate into teaching practice, Brian Street does suggest that the social practice view of literacy requires 'an emphasis on real uses of literacy and attention to the contexts of use' (*ibid.*: 85). It is sometimes easier in teaching to present archetypal texts, such as sets of instructions or other genres that comply with standard sets of distinctive linguistic features. In many ways this is the danger of a genre approach to literacy. While texts do fit into genres and may often exhibit some grammatical aspects that allow them to be grouped in this way, language is more complex than a standardised list of genre characteristics might suggest. It is far better to start with a real text and enable learners to analyse it for the features of a particular genre. This works on both the learner's language analysis skills while acknowledging that real texts aren't as neat as we may have been led to believe in school.

A social practice view of literacy requires that we see beyond the literacy event and the skills involved in that event to the practices that surround it. Let's go back to the letter writing example. It's not enough to teach a group of learners how to write a formal letter, without first exploring:

- *if and when they do this already*

- *if they are involved in formal letter writing with someone else offering support*

- *how they might use a formal letter once they have learned how to write one*

- *any experiences when a formal letter would have been useful*

- *how they react to a formal letter and how they respond.*

Unless we explore how a letter might have meaning for the learner, the skills of formal letter writing don't have a social context and are unlikely to transfer from the classroom to the learner's own context. We can tick off the 'target' when the letter has been produced in class, but would have to question whether that learner now sees herself as a letter writer.

While it's important to start with real texts, it is also important to think about how we go beyond that literacy event to a set of literacy practices. Why would we write this particular letter? If we take a workplace setting, we might be writing to confirm a problem with an order. If we follow through the whole series of communication events that lead to the letter we might have:

- *reading documentation and checking shipment*

- *reading original order to check if it matches shipment*

- *phoning supplier to query problem*

- *writing letter that puts that telephone conversation into writing as proof of that conversation*

In this sequence, the letter has meaning as it has a context. Why not use the simulation of events and strings of events in the literacy classroom? While working on the separate skills and literacy formats can develop individual skills, role playing a whole sequence gives the skills their context within literacy practices. They become meaningful.

Practical idea 2

There are a number of difficulties inherent in teaching letter writing, or any other genre in literacy. We know that literacy practices change. As seen in the earlier student discussion, students in this group don't write, and have no plans to write, informal letters. However, group discussion did lead to a number of ways in which formal letters played a part in their lives.

- **Letter layout** – a discussion on this may not achieve consensus. It seems to depend on whether the speaker has been trained in typing or word-processing, (where they may have learnt a prescriptive notion of layout) and when their training had taken place. Those who have been taught by other teachers may also feel that handwritten letters have distinctive features, such as indented paragraphs.

- **Letter collection** – collect formal letters over a number of weeks. This could provide enough evidence to inform the group that, for example, the date can go in any number of places.

- **Practical tips** – the group can agree what has to be included in a formal letter, such as:

  - Your postal address

  - Their address

  - Date

  - A formal style of address to the person being written to (Dear Mr … rather than Hi there)

  - The writing has to be formal and spelling and presentation are important

  - You have to include your name clearly at the bottom and write it near your signature if this is not clear

There are other things to include where appropriate, such as:

- Reference number of some sort

- Your telephone or e-mail contact details if you want someone to contact you that way

These are not the only choices. We may put the postal address where we want at the top of the letter. The important thing is to put it in.

After carrying out this activity with one group of learners, I found that when we revisited letter writing months later in this class they immediately recalled the list of items that must be included in a formal letter. Perhaps this discovery learning gave them ownership. More importantly it allowed them to practice the analytical skills that could be used in another situation.

In many ways it is more comfortable for us as teachers and learners to have set structures that we learn about the language. But adults aren't children. The minute you tell someone not to start sentences with 'but' they will bring in something by Dickens where he did exactly that. It is far better to work with your learners exploring the English language, however complex, to arrive at a better understanding for everyone. As Brian Street put it, 'The emphasis from this perspective, then, is on appropriateness … rather than on a pure concept of correctness that dominates much formal thinking on language and literacy' (*ibid.*:85).

In this book we don't offer lots of answers and well-developed ideas for the classroom. Rather, we call for further research with learners into how we all use literacy, how literacy practices are changing and how we and they can achieve change in literacy practices. It's a call for all teachers to be researchers in the classroom; not in order to publish, but in order to reflect on and improve teaching. It's a call for all students to be involved in that research, as partners not as objects.

Appendix 1

Training for research

Jane Mace

As we said in the introduction, the work in this book originated as an assignment task set for an adult literacy teacher's qualification course. Between the two of us, we have at the time of writing taught the assignment with five different groups of trainee teachers. In each case, the task itself remained essentially the same. What we found we needed to develop was the guidance we gave for it. We learned something about making explicit the expectations behind it. We realised we needed to spell out some differences between preparing to teach and preparing to research. We worked out one or two strategies to make these expectations explicit and spell out these differences. In this appendix I set out five of these, in the hope they could be useful to others: three texts and two activities:

- the assignment brief

- an exercise to practice interviewing

- guidance on the structure of report.

- the 'five finger exercise'

- peer presentations and feedback.

1. The assignment brief

This is the most recent version of the text that was given to participants. It has been amended several times and may well be again.

The task: a 2000-word report on literacy as a social practice and its implications for adult literacy teaching and learning, illustrated by a case study.

The criteria for assessment:

Your report will need to show your ability to:

- explain the social practice view of adult literacy for a general reader, making reference to sources as appropriate;

- apply one or more of the related concepts of domain, roles and networks to a specific case;

- provide an account of one learner's literacy events outside the classroom context, as reported by the learner or observed by you;

- produce a well-structured report of research undertaken, providing justification for any observations or new insights.

Reading: For this assignment, the reading load is light but needs to be thoughtful. You should show evidence of having consulted between two and four relevant sources and provide some reflective reference to these (as indicated in the outcomes).

Case study: The main work for this assignment is in setting up what is in effect a mini-research project. Your aim is to document, analyse and reflect on the social reality which forms the context for someone who is currently an adult learner of literacy. They could be one of your own students, or one that a colleague has introduced you to.

You need to allow time to:

- find, get the agreement of, and meet the person concerned twice (once for research interview, and a second time for you to give feedback and them to provide further reflection/amendments to anything they have said);

- work out some appropriate questions and method of recording answers (there will be input in course time on this); reflect on the insights you have gained from these

- research and record something of their literacy environment;

- reflect on the connections between your findings and relevant course reading.

The finished report:

This should include

- your thinking about the social practice theory of literacy with reference to relevant reading

- an account of how you set about your investigation (your methods) with what expectations or 'hunches';

- what you learned about the learner's reality, using their own words as appropriate (ensuring use of pseudonym if required);

- your reflections on the implications this study has raised for you about teaching approaches.

Guidelines on collecting and using data

1. Finding the learner

You could put the idea to a class you teach and ask for a volunteer; or

you could approach a learner you know or enlist the help of a colleague to identify someone they think would be willing.

2. Explaining the idea

It will be important to stress this is to be a conversation about their life, not their skills; (this is not a teacher assessing abilities but a researcher seeking to learn about the person). You'll need to explain the idea of a) literacy events and b) networks, giving examples.

3. The data

Ask that they first write a short pen sketch of themselves (with you as scribe if that feels best). e.g.

> *My name is Rosa. I've lived in this part of Coleford for ten years now. My kids are grown up and I give a hand with the youngest grandchild. I work as a cleaner in the council offices.*

Ask that they include a couple of sentences which describe their interests (eg I very much enjoy …; or on Thursday evenings I always …) and their aspirations in relation to literacy (e.g. I've recently taken on … and I'd like to be able to deal with the paperwork rather than relying on my friend).

4. The literacy environment

Record what you can of 'Rosa's' literacy environment: the literacy events or episodes that she has said are likely to occur for her in her local area or workplace. Be detailed. If Rosa tells you of an interest in, for example, sport, you could invite her to take photographs of any literacy events involved and discuss these together. Collect and study any texts you find that relate to her context. If you discuss the look or the content of a text in any detail, include this as an appendix.

5. Ethics

Make sure Rosa knows that this is a report, not a published piece, and that if she would prefer, you could refer to her with a pseudonym of her choice.

Lastly, remember, in your essay, to be clear whether what you are saying about Rosa's reality is something that Rosa herself has said or whether it is something that you have observed or surmised about her.

2. Interview practice exercise

We found that teachers need encouraging to see this kind of interview work as different from the interviews they usually do – at initial meetings with new learners, for example. In order to give proper thought to the interviewee's experience, we designed a role play activity which drew on edited versions of some case studies in this book.

People had to work in pairs. They were given a brief profile on their imagined interviewee to take away. The profile contained gaps; it was their task to fill these in and, as it were, put themselves in the shoes of that person. The following week, everyone took a turn to be both interviewer and interviewee. Several useful things emerged. As interviewer, people felt diffident and concerned about being intrusive. As interviewee, people found that they were not entirely clear of the purpose of the questions. Again, some interviewers found their interviewees talked non-stop and went off on tangents; while others had to deal with monosyllabic responses and long pauses. Afterwards, the group discussed concerns such as: how to show polite interest in what is being said, even if it is 'off the point' of the interview.

The following is the text of the brief sheet given along with the profile sheet:

Preparation for role play exercise in Session 2.
There will be two exercises; one, where you play the interviewee;
the second, where you practise being the interviewer.
In preparation for the session, think about the notes below and fill in some notes on the person profile attached. Keep this profile to yourself until next week.

Interviewee

You will be playing the person in the case study.

Your role is to help the interviewer practise their skills.

Think of the thoughts you have had about the person and what literacy activity this may mean they engage in.

'Ad lib' as you like – for example, about friends or family they may turn to for literacy purposes – but keep to the basic outline of the person.

Help the interviewer practise their skills by not coming out with all the information you have (but they don't) at the start.

Give thought to how you might feel about the questions being asked.

Interviewer

Your aim is to learn from the interviewee.

Your first task is to clarify the purpose of the interview.

All you know so far is their name and the fact that they are a learner in a basic skills class.

What you seek to know, is something of their literacy life outside the classroom: how reading and writing turns up in other parts of their lives, who they work with to deal with it, and what their literacy interests may be in one or other of these various contexts.

Prepare: a few possible questions to get things going; questions that may help with this inquiry;

one or two things you can say to clarify your purpose;

and something you could say as to how you will use what they tell you.

Remember: the focus is on interests, community life, and/or work first Questions about literacy follow, as in: "so, does reading or writing crop up for you at all in doing that?"

Each summarised profile provided for 'interviewees' began with the words: "read through the profile and, using your imagination, fill in the blanks/boxes" – which were the following:

How everyday mail gets dealt with in your household
How letters to family get written
Literacy events that crop up for you (and any changes)
Your feelings about this interview Before:
Your feelings about this interview During: (fill this in after the interview)

These are two examples of the edited profiles that followed:

1. You are Dave. Single, in your early 30s, you live alone in a small modern house. You have a brother who is successful in business, married, with children; your parents, who you see regularly, live the other side of town.

You have two main hobbies: .... and .... You keep a scrapbook on the former and go along to meetings of the local group to share enthusiasms/go on outings/listen to speakers (delete as appropriate!) on the latter.

You left school at 15 to train to become a .... This involved you coming to college for one day each week, but you were made redundant after two years. You then got a job with Tesco, shelf-filling. As you had difficulty reading the labels you were moved to the 'back door' where the goods are delivered. You were having trouble reading the documents before signing them. Your manager fixed up an interview for you at the college to start basic skills literacy classes.

2. You are Paula: .... years old, married with .... children; interested in the life of your village. When the kids were small, you worked part-time work as a carer and home-help for the elderly and became chairperson of the local .... At that time, you weren't much bothered about any spelling problems you had, but as the kids have got older you have become more self-conscious. (When they ask for help with their homework you'd say things like, 'Go and ask your dad, he's better than me at that,' or 'I haven't got the time' and you'd get on with yet more housework.)

Not long ago, you joined the local .... One day in Bible reading class, the leader asked for a volunteer to read aloud. When she asked you, you declined. After the class the leader took you on one side and explained that her son was dyslexic and that she had suspected that you might be too. She made the initial contact for you to attend a basic skills class.

Not everyone relishes the prospect of role play; some course participants raise objections to the idea of doing it. However, an important argument in its favour is that without this chance to practise interviews of this kind, the research interview is effectively being done by an untrained interviewer. The resulting interview may not only fail to open up new insights, but also be a poor experience for the interviewee.

As research interviewers, we all need training to remind us how it feels to be on the other side of an interview. We need to keep fresh in their minds, too, the need to make a space for interviewees to describe their interests or identities outside any list of questions that we may have prepared beforehand.

This is how one course participant reflected on the experience:

I had not been looking forward to this session. I'm sceptical about the value of role-play. However, this was one occasion on which my prejudices were proved wrong. It was difficult to get over the artificiality of the process, but I did discover how important it is to be sensitive to the interviewee and to hear what they are not telling you, as much as what they are.

Liz, who interviewed me, was excellent in her manner and her follow-up questioning, picking up on things I said, as 'Paula'. However, I did make it hard for her, having decided that I would be a bit defensive and reticent. I found myself thinking my way into my character and desperately wanting Liz to ask me questions about what I did with myself (possibly not in those words!) since I had given up work. I had decided I was a fantastic gardener and cook, providing fresh vegetables, fruit and cakes for half the village, but during the interview I felt I couldn't say all this unless there was a question that would 'let me in' to this information. Since there was no opportunity, I left it unsaid. I felt that I had come over as someone with problems who had not been able to cope with form-filling and that there was more to me than that.

It did make me realise how important it was to find the right questions as an interviewer and being aware of areas that had not been touched on which might alter the interviewer's perception of the interviewee.[1]

3. Guidance on writing the report

Along with the assignment brief, it was important to spell out what kind of writing was being expected of participants when they came to 'write up' their case study. Such a report is, after all, a different genre of writing from an essay. The writer has to explain something of what they did and why: there needs to be some relationship made between their findings and those of other studies. Like anyone undertaking such work as part of graduate research course, these researchers (working at undergraduate level) benefited from proper guidance about this writing (a better idea than us leaving them having to guess their way into it). Here is what we came up with:

Outline of report

Your report needs to include the following:

Title: Literacy as a social practice: the case of [Rosa] (name/pseudonym of your subject)

Introduction: Statement of research question, your interest in/attitude to it, and broad structure of the report

Situating sections:

- *theory/research: your understanding of this, with appropriate ref(s)*

- *practice/learning context of your meeting with subject*

---

[1]   Janette Denyer, Cirencester College; reproduced with permission from *Learning and Teaching Journal*, September 2004

Methodology:

- *how you explored your question interview/s pen sketch researching something of the subject's literacy environment*

Findings and analysis:

- *picture of the person that you have got to know*
- *particular literacy event/s that s/he deals with*
- *your comment on domain, network and/or roles involved*

Conclusion (re-situating)

- *how your findings connect with the theory you have found*
- *what you can say now about the question you were exploring*
- *any insights for the practice/learning context*

It's a good idea to use sub-headings. 'Introduction' and 'conclusion' are useful ones to keep as they are; for the middle three sections of the piece (situating the project, methods, findings), choose your own wording.

4. The 'five finger exercise'

Before attempting a full performance piece, a pianist does some warming up – sometimes with what used to be called 'five finger exercises'. In creative writing courses, participants are often invited to do a piece of 'free writing': write without taking your pen off the page, they are told. Do not listen to the voice of your inner critic. Get your hand moving – and create some material you can work with.

With this assignment (as with others) teacher-researchers stand to benefit from a mix of these two approaches. Warming up to the task of writing something about theory; and writing without self-censorship their own version of what they think that theory is.

The 'five finger exercise' consists in asking them to pick up their pens and spend five minutes, there and then, doing that: writing in their own words what they understood to be the social practice view of literacy.

This invitation can cause some alarm. It helps to clarify that no-one else will be reading it but the writer. Pens gradually begin to move. Following the exercise, people can be invited to share what they have written by reading it out. There can be surprises for them in how the act of drafting an idea in our own words enables us to give it new expression. Here is a good example from Chris Cox, an experienced adult literacy teacher in Bristol:

A social practice view of adult literacy means taking a step back from our practice as teachers in order to learn from students of literacy. It means giving ourselves permission to question assumptions, statistics, analysis by government and others and to refocus on the real experiences of real people.

In her job Chris managed and taught a programme of adult literacy and basic skills classes; producing records of planning, delivering, evaluating and assessing learning which, in turn, would be used (in statistical returns) for the funding of her organisation. Taking a step back from this framework of reference, as she saw it, freed her to look with a fresh eye at the 'real experiences of real people': people whose literacy activity was usually captured only in terms of classroom achievement.

5. Peer presentations and feedback

Of all the strategies we used in work on this area of the course, the single most useful one, which stands out for both of us more than any other, was that of enabling participants to talk about their own work in progress and listen to each other's.

Putting things in words, in conversation, helps us to think, explore, make knowledge ours. Speaking about ideas we are working on to an interested audience provides us with the chance to get some sense of whether these ideas make sense to anyone else. Listeners can offer us questions. We discover we have left out something which was obvious to us. We gain additional ideas worth exploring further. All this, of course, depends on listeners agreeing in the first place to respond in the spirit of support and collaboration: recognising the first principle of good feedback – before you say anything else, say something positive about what you have heard. Only then, ask questions for clarification or make suggestions on what else needs doing.

To make such feedback effective, the session has to be fairly firmly structured. People need to have the confidence that they will have an amount of time and attention which is equal to that which others are having. Time-keeping must therefore be of the essence. Similarly, speakers being asked questions about what they have said benefit from having someone taking a note for them – not recording the answers they gave, as much as the questions they were asked. Taking these notes home can help bring back to mind the thinking that went on as they were working out how to answer the question: thinking which could help the work itself grow and be intelligible to the eventual reader.

Appendix 2: Permission request

Reading, writing and everyday life

We find that there are a lot of mistaken ideas about how people can't manage reading and writing unless they are very good at literacy. The idea of this book is to show a different set of pictures. We would like the book to include the research that you helped your tutor to do, including your pen portrait of yourself.

We think these pieces of writing are important and special. The reason we think so is that they are about what people really do with reading and writing in everyday life. As we see it, the book could help improve the understanding, not only of teachers like those who did the research, but of all sorts of other people too.

At the moment we don't have a publishing contract, but we think it is important that you know about this idea and are willing to have your work included.

We are seeking your agreement to a number of things we would like you to think about.

Please let us know your wishes by filling in the form below. We will keep in touch with your tutor about how we get on after that and make sure that you get a chance to check the case study before publication.

Thank you.

Ellayne Fowler and Jane Mace

November 2003

_____

Your name _____

Tutor's name _____

Please tick if you agree for us to use:

- Case study as written by tutor
- Pen portrait as written by you

(If there is anything you would like to add to your pen portrait, please talk about this with your tutor and give the changes to her to send to us)

Can you also tick one of these:

- You can use my first name

- I would like you not to use my name, but this pen name:

Signed _____ Date:_____

Bibliography

Barton, D. (1994) *Literacy: an introduction to the ecology of written language*, London: Routledge

Barton, D. and Hamilton M. (1998) *Local literacies: reading and writing in one community*, London: Routledge

Barton, D., Hamilton, M. and Ivanič, R. (2000) (eds) *Situated literacies: reading and writing in context*, London: Routledge

Barton, D. and Padmore, S. (1994) 'Roles, Networks and Values in Everyday Writing' in Graddol, D., Maybin, J. and Stierer, B. (eds) *Researching Language and Literacy in Social Context*. Clevedon: Multilingual Matters

Basic Skills Agency (2001) *Adult literacy core curriculum*, DfES

Boland, E. (1996) *Object lessons: the life of the woman and the poet in our time*, London: Vintage

Bourdieu, P. (1991) *Language and Symbolic Power*. Cambridge, Harvard University Press

Bucholtz, M. (2003) '"Why be normal?": Language and identity practices in a community of nerd girls' in Goodman, S., Lillis, T., Maybin, J. and Mercer, N. (eds) *Language, Literacy and Education: A Reader*, Stoke on Trent: Trentham Books Ltd

Cameron, D. et al (1992) *Researching language: issues of power and method*, London: Routledge

Castleton, G. (2001) 'The role of literacy in people's lives: a case study of its use amongst the homeless in Australia' in Crowther, J., Hamilton, M. and Tett, L. (eds) *Powerful literacies*, Leicester: NIACE

Clanchy, M. (1979) From memory to written record: England 1066–1307, London: Edward Arnold

Cox, C. (2004) A social practice view of literacy: first draft of unpublished essay for Level 4 certificate course, Bristol

Crowther, J., Hamilton, M. and Tett, L. (eds) (2001) *Powerful literacies*, Leicester, NIACE

Davies, L. (1985) 'Ethnography and status: focussing on gender in educational research', in Burgess, R., *Field methods in the study of education*, London: Falmer Press

Davies, P. (1994) 'Long term unemployment and literacy: a case study of the Restart interview' in: Hamilton, M., Barton, D. and Ivanič, R., *Worlds of Literacy*, Clevedon: Multilingual Matters

Denscombe, M. (1998) *The Good Research Guide*, Maidenhead: Open University Press

Fawns, M. and Ivanič, R. (2001) 'Form-filling as a social practice: taking power into our own hands' in: Crowther, J., Hamilton, M. and Tett, L. op cit

FENTO (2002) Subject specifications for teachers of adult literacy and numeracy, Department of Education and Science/Readwriteplus

Fingeret, A. (1983) 'Social Network: A new perspective on independence and illiterate adults' in *Adult Education Quarterly* 33: page numbers 133–46

Fishman, J.A. (1989) *Language and Ethnicity in Minority Sociolinguistic Perspective*, Clevedon: Mulitilingual Matters Ltd

Freire, P. (1994) 'The Adult Literacy Process as Cultural Action for Freedom' in Maybin, J. (ed) *Language and Literacy in Social Practice*, Clevedon: Multilingual Matters Ltd

Gee, J. (1990) *Social linguistics and literacies: ideology in discourse*, London: The Falmer Press

Hamilton, M. (2000) 'Expanding the new literacy studies: using photographs to explore literacy as social practice' in Barton, D., Hamilton, M., and Ivanič, R. (2000) (eds) *Situated literacies: reading and writing in context*, London: Routledge

Hamilton, M., Macrae, C., and Tett, L., (eds) (2001) "Powerful Literacies: the Policy Context" in Crowther, Hamilton and Tett, op cit

Hammersley, M. (1994) Introducing ethnography, in: Graddol, D., Maybin, J. and Stierer, B. (eds) *Researching language and literacy in social context*, Clevedon: Multilingual Matters/The Open University

Heath, S.B. (1994) 'What No Bedtime Story Means: Narrative Skills at Home and School' in Maybin, J. (ed) *Language and Literacy in Social Practice*, Clevedon: Multilingual Matters Ltd

Holmes, J. (2001) 2nd ed. *An Introduction to Sociolinguistics*, Harlow: Pearson Education Ltd

Ivanič, R. (1998) *Writing and Identity*, Amsterdam: John Benjamins

Labov, W. (1972) *Sociolinguistic Patterns*, Oxford: Basil Blackwell

Lave, J. and Wenger, E. (1991) *Situated Learning: Legitimate peripheral Participation*, Cambridge: Cambridge University Press

Lavender, P. (2004) 'Tests, targets and ptarmigans' in: Lavender, P., Derrick, J. and Brooks, B., *Testing, testing ... 1, 2, 3*, Leicester, NIACE

Mace, J. (1992) *Talking about literacy: principles and practice of adult literacy Education*, London: Routledge

Mace, J. (1998) *Playing with time: mothers and the meaning of literacy*, London: Routledge/UCL Press

Mace, J. (2001) 'Signatures and the lettered world' in: Crowther, Hamilton and Tett op cit

Mace, J. (2002) *The Give and Take of Writing: Scribes, literacy and everyday Life*, Leicester: NIACE

Mace, J. (2004) 'Language experience: what's going on?' *Literacy Today*, June: 6. (accessible via: www.literacytrust.org.uk)

Milroy, L. (1987) 2nd ed. *Language and Social Networks*, Oxford: Blackwell Publishers

Moser, C. (1999) *A fresh Start: improving literacy and numeracy*, DFEE

National Literacy Trust (2004) *Key milestones in the development of adult basic skills 1993–2003* www.literacytrust.org.uk/database/basicskillstimeline.html

NRDC (n.d.) *Strategy 2003–2007: generating knowledge and transforming it into practice*, National Research and Development Centre

Organisation for Economic Cooperation and Development (2000) *Literacy in The Information Age*, Paris: OECD

Rahman, A. MD (1993) *People's self-development*, London: Zed Books

RaPAL (2005) website: www.lancaster.ac.uk/literacy

Saxena, M. (1993) 'Literacies among the Panjabis' in Southall in Maybin, J (ed) *Language and Literacy in Social Practice*, Clevedon: Multilingual Matters/ Open University

Street, B. (1993) (ed) *Cross-cultural approaches to literacy*, Cambridge: Cambridge University Press

Street, B. (1994) 'Cross-cultural Perspectives on Literacy' in Maybin, J. (ed) *Language and Literacy in Social Practice*, Clevedon: Multilingual Matters and Open University

Street, B. (1995) *Social literacies: critical approaches to literacy in development, ethnography and education*, London: Longman

Street, B. (2001) 'Contexts for literacy work: the "new orders" and the "new literacy studies" ' in Crowther, J., Hamilton, M., Tett, L. (eds) *Powerful Literacies*, Leicester: NIACE

Street, B. (2003) 'The implications of the "New Literacy Studies" for literacy education' in Goodman, S., Lillis, T., Maybin, J. and Mercer, N. (eds) *Language, Literacy and Education*: A Reader, Stoke on Trent: Trentham Books Ltd

Taylor, D. (1998) *Family Literacy: young children learning to read and write*, London: Heinemann

Tomlin, A. (2004) 'How can we get critical feedback from students?', in *Reflect*, issue one, National Research and Development Centre for adult literacy and numeracy

Tusting, K., Ivanič, R. and Wilson, A. (2000) 'New Literacy Studies at the Interchange' in Barton, D., Hamilton, M. and Ivanič, R. (2000) (eds) *Situated literacies: reading and writing in context*, London: Routledge

Ward, J. and Edwards, J. (2002) *Learning journeys: learners' voices: research report*, Learning Skills Development Agency

Wenger, E. (1998) *Communities of Practice: Learning, Meaning, and Identity*, Cambridge: Cambridge University Press

Wilkinson, P. (2003) *Christianity*, London: Eyewitness Guides

Wilson, A. (2003) 'Researching in the Third Space: locating, claiming and valuing the research domain' in Goodman, S., Lillis, T., Maybin, J. and Mercer, N. (eds) *Language, Literacy and Education: A Reader*, Stoke on Trent: Trentham Books Ltd

Yule, G. (1996) *The study of language*, Cambridge: Cambridge University Press (2nd ed.)

Contributors

Karen Bell

Karen left school having achieved only an English O Level, having hated every minute of it. Once she'd started a family, Karen realised she could relate well to individuals who had experienced troubled times at school who left school unable to read or write to their full potential. She began as a volunteer tutor in 1996 and now leads the LLN team at Cirencester College teaching literacy as well as tutor training.

Karen Bilous

Karen first became aware of adult literacy over 15 years ago when working in adult and community learning. She became a volunteer and went on to qualify as a literacy tutor, eventually becoming Basic Skills Co-ordinator at Gloscat for seven years, delivering basic skills teacher training. Karen has recently returned to adult and community learning as Head of Learning Programmes for Gloucestershire with a remit which includes targeting the most disadvantaged learners across the county for both discrete and embedded basic skills courses.

Susan Buchanan

While teaching IT to disadvantaged adults, Susan was very aware that many of the learners had basic literacy needs and decided to train as a basic skills tutor on a pilot training scheme. For the past two years she has worked as a full-time tutor in the Essential Skills department at Salisbury College, teaching literacy, learning support and numeracy. Working with adults in adult basic education is the most fulfilling role Susan has ever had in a lifetime spent in education.

Sarah Chu

Sarah taught English as a foreign language at a university in China and Business English in Shanghai before returning to England in 2001, where she moved into teaching English for Speakers of Other Languages (ESOL) in East London before moving to Wiltshire College in 2002. She is the programme leader for Outreach ABE and ESOL and also delivers part of the teacher training at Level 2 and 4. Sarah's main background is in ESOL but she is also involved in literacy.

Ellayne Fowler

Ellayne works as a teacher and teacher-trainer at Wiltshire College and as an associate lecturer for the Open University. Her research interest is in literacy as a social practice and, in particular, how to translate that approach into classroom practice. Ellayne has worked in the adult literacy field in the UK and the USA in a wide range of contexts and is a past chair of RaPAL.

Claire Griffin

Claire works at Filton College in Bristol as Learning Area Manager for Basic Skills. She has been in adult basic education since 1976, working as a teacher and organiser in a range of contexts. She is also an experienced regional teacher-trainer, currently teaching Levels 2, 3 and 4 in adult literacy at Filton.

Mig Holder

Mig has spent all her working life in community outreach and adult learning, teaching creative writing, textiles, embroidery and literacy, and for five years until 2004, being the Essential Skills Curriculum Manager at Weston-super-Mare College. She is now a trainer on Level 3/4 Literacy Subject Support and Specialist courses and is developing a community learning centre in Derby. She is passionate about the changes that literacy learning and development can make to individuals' lives.

Tricia Jones

Tricia is a teacher and teacher-trainer for Bath Adult and Community Education Department. Her role as organiser of one-to-one supported learning for vulnerable students has led to a special interest in adult dyslexia and other learning difficulties. Tricia has worked with adult learners in a wide variety of contexts, both academic and commercial.

Gillian Knox

Gillian Knox works at Swindon College and is Pathway Leader for Maths and English Development. She has ten years experience of teaching adult learners in the college and community and has also taught within the Probation Service and on family learning programmes. She has tutored on the Level 4 teacher training programme (literacy) and is lead trainer for the Level 2 Certificate in Adult Learner Support.

Sarah Lyster

Sarah started teaching basic skills literacy in a prison before moving to work with Dorset Adult Education Service teaching both literacy and ESOL. She is passionate about enabling people to enrich their lives through an improved understanding of language.

Kauser McCallum

Kauser McCallum has been working in basic skills and ESOL since 1979. She is currently working as a part-time basic skills tutor at Swindon College and a part-time consultant with the Evaluation Trust.

Jane Mace

Jane is a consultant in adult literacy and community education, with experience as teacher, manager, editor and author. A founder member of the Research and Practice in Adult Literacy (RaPAL) network, her interests are in the creative tension between spoken and written language: a theme which recurs in her books (see Bibliography). She currently teaches on courses in adult literacy studies for Lancaster University, City of Bristol College and the Institute of Education, London.

Liz McKee

Liz came late to teaching, after a varied career. She currently teaches adult literacy, numeracy and learning support at Salisbury College. Liz finds the work inspirational and satisfying.

Sheila Nicholson

Sheila teaches learning skills at City of Bath College where she has also contributed to delivering the Level 2 Certificate in Adult Learner Support. In addition, she works as a community education tutor teaching literacy to adults and has recently become involved in family learning.

Haoli Rein

Haoli works as Basic Skills Co-ordinator for Swindon College, promoting essential skills training to employers. She also teaches literacy courses to adults in the workplace and is particularly interested in how language is affected by social context.

Sue Thain

Sue has worked with members of the Armed Forces and their families for over 25 years. During that time she has travelled extensively and taught a wide variety of subjects in diverse locations. She is currently employed in the Directorate of Education and Training Services (Army) developing and implementing an Army specific basic skills awareness training package and mentor scheme based around the Level 2 Adult Learner Support qualification.

Kate Tomlinson

Kate started in adult basic education in 1976, at first as a volunteer and then Area Organiser for the LEA scheme in Gloucestershire and since 1990 as a tutor/tutor trainer for Stroud College of FE where she has worked ever since. Kate's main interest has been in student writing and she has enjoyed participating in writing workshops both in the UK and abroad.

Chris Topham

Chris is currently working with adult learners (over 50) to improve their literacy skills and confidence. In this she draws on a lifetime's interest in language learning (researched as student, teacher, parent and now grandparent) and her enthusiasm for learning languages (including Swedish, a smattering of Welsh and some Faroese). Her career includes 20 years classroom experience in Middle School, specialising in Maths and French.

Mandy Weatherett

Mandy has spent 20 years working in Africa, Asia and Europe as an English teacher and language coordinator. She is now teaching literacy, ESOL and communication skills for a community-based training company in Swindon. In addition to teaching, Mandy has also written embedded literacy material for the awarding body ASDAN.

Gill Whalley

Gill Whalley works as a senior tutor in family learning for Wakefield adult Education authotity and as an Associate Lecturer for the Open University. She has worked in the field of adult and community education, in many different contexts, for 15 years.

Jackie Winchcombe

Jackie came into adult basic education later than most having discovered an interest in adult literacy while working for a confidential advice centre. She started as a volunteer and now works as a literacy teacher for both The Learning

Curve and Wiltshire College, Calne. Since qualifying she has developed a special interest in working with learners on Probation orders and has recently additionally taken on the post of Probation Contracts Co-ordinator for The Learning Curve.

Index

Index

cultural communities 106
cultural identity 35, 37, 106
cultural structures 10
cultural tradition 71
data collection 117
Dave – case study 18–21
Decreolization 67
deficit model 76, 101, 106
dense networks 26–7, 36, 58, 91, 93–4
diagnostic assessment 75, 110
diagrammatic presentations 18, 23
domains 42, 48, 52–4, 56, 72, 116
drafting 122
dyslexia 39, 41, 60–1, 89, 91, 105
Eckert, Penelope 29
economic activity 109
education domain 30–1, 49, 53, 107, 108, 109
Education and Skills, Department for – DfES
    viii–ix
Edwards, Judith 77
e-mail 111
employment 14, 22
empowerment 76–9
English
    Jamaican 67
    Standard 67, 74
    ESOL 35
    Creole 67
ESOL (English for Speakers of Other
    Languages) classes 35
essays 53–4, 56
ethical research 77
ethics 117
ethnicity 24, 26
ethnography 75–6
evidence 2, 3–6, 8, 23
expertise 103–4
eye contact 95
family 22, 30, 47, 49, 52–3, 76, 79
feedback 82, 105, 109, 116, 123
Fingeret, Arlene 27, 48, 61, 104, 106
Fishman, Joshua 49
five-finger exercise 122–3
formal letters 10, 13, 22, 57, 112–14
form-filling 5–6, 103
Fowler, Ellayne 100, 142
Freire, Paulo 68
funding 6
Further Education National Training
    Organisation – FENTO x
gender 10, 22, 24, 26, 29
graffiti 55
grammar 24, 34
Griffin, Claire 45, 105, 107, 109, 142
groups, membership of 25

Hamilton, Mary ix, 29, 50, 52, 82
Heath, S.B. 54
Holder, Mig 80, 82, 94, 101, 142
Holmes, Janet 49
home domain 10, 53–5, 110
homelessness 28
identity 2, 73, 101, 105–7, 108
ideology 71
idiolect 24
illiteracy 3, 27, 38
images 20–1, 62
imagination 83
immigration 99
individual language use 24–25
inequality 76
inference 102
informal letters 17, 102
initial assessment 110–11
interaction 52, 55
International Adult Literacy Survey – IALS 38
interviews 80–3, 118–21
Irene – case study 69–73
Ivanič, Roz 8
Jamaican English 67
jargon 11
Jed – case study 83–5
Job Centres 5
John – case study (1) 11–15
John – case study (2) 85–8
Jones, Tricia 9, 80, 142
Joyce – case study 40–4
Knox, Gillian 40, 48, 81, 104, 106, 142
Labels 105–7
language
    analysis 112
    Creole 67
    decreolization 67
    formality 111
    individual use of 24–5
    interaction 24
    meta-language 49
    phonics 21
    pitch 24
    pronunciation 24
    region 24
    social aspects 25, 29
    social class 24
    spoken 1–2, 8, 23, 24–5, 82, 99
    structures 114
    technical 22
    tone 24
    use 224
    variety 25
    vocabulary 24
    written 1–2, 3–4, 5–8, 23, 107–8

138

Index